SING EMMANUEL

By the same author (with Simon Webley)

LOUD AND CLEAR

SING EMMANUEL

The story of Edwin Shepherd and the London Emmanuel Choir

by JOHN CAPON

WORD BOOKS
LONDON
and Waco, Texas, U.S.A.

WORD BOOKS
Park Lane
Hemel Hempstead
Hertfordshire

First published October 1971
Second printing December 1971

ISBN 0 85009 031 8

Printed and bound in Great Britain by
Hazell Watson & Viney Ltd,
Aylesbury, Bucks.

FOREWORD

It is a great privilege, in a brief foreword, to pay my tribute to Edwin Shepherd and to the great choir which he and his beloved wife Muriel formed and maintained for so many years. We are so grateful to God that under the leadership of Muriel the choir lives on – and so will the life of Edwin live in our memories for he was loved by everyone.

The London Emmanuel Choir is a great evangelistic force wherever it goes. I can testify to this because I must have accompanied the choir to give the closing message on more than 100 occasions. Edwin always spoke with great power and could have done this himself, but he graciously made way for me.

What was the secret of the great spiritual message of the choir? You had only to hear Edwin's prayer before choir practice began, and you have the answer. His consuming purpose in life was to give his best to God and this book unfolds the fascinating story of the choir and its leader as they ventured out in God's service. I know Edwin would wish that God should get the glory.

Dr. F. B. Meyer was a great friend of mine, and on his tombstone are the words 'The man who reckoned upon God'. Edwin Shepherd was another man who brings this phrase to my mind.

A. LINDSAY GLEGG

ILLUSTRATIONS

ILLUSTRATIONS

Between pages 32 and 33

[illegible]
[illegible] Shepherd [illegible] by Arthur Charles and [illegible]
[illegible]
[illegible]
Edward and [illegible] 1961
[illegible] Road [illegible]
[illegible] the London [illegible] Christ 1946
[illegible] picture [illegible] London [illegible] 1970

Between pages 96 and 97

[illegible] of life
[illegible] and Smith and George Beverly Shea [illegible]
[illegible] with George Beverly Shea [illegible]
Volunteers [illegible] the [illegible] forms [illegible] Crusade
The 1,500-voice choir at the Royal Albert Hall [illegible] a concert [illegible] the Fourth Festival of [illegible] Evangelical [illegible] Churches [illegible] 1970
[illegible]

AUTHOR'S NOTE

This book was written in a hurry. I say that not to excuse its inadequacies but to underline my indebtedness to the people without whose willing and speedy assistance it could not have been written at all.

My thanks must go first to Muriel Shepherd who not only spent many hours talking to me on tape but also made available to me countless letters, personal papers, press cuttings and photographs concerning her husband and the choir.

Then to Miss Caroline Johnson, of the *Christian Herald*, I am most grateful for permission to draw freely upon material contained in an unpublished manuscript about the choir she compiled in 1966.

The following have assisted me in diverse ways and to all of them I extend my gratitude: Mr. and Mrs. Charles Shepherd, Miss Ann Spredbury, Messrs. Norman Preston, Colin Haughton, Raymond Moseley, Frank Waller, Frank Birkenshaw, Douglas Lawson and Miss Pat Thomas.

Then of course there are the members of the London Emmanuel Choir who have given me interviews, written numerous letters and inundated me with anecdotes, press clippings and photographs. It would be invidious to single out individual choir members; to all those who have so readily come forward to offer assistance I express my grateful thanks.

I could almost include Mr. Lindsay Glegg as a choir member, so often does he share a platform with them, but of course he is not. There could not be a more suitable person to write the foreword, however, and I am grateful to him for agreeing to do so.

My thanks must also go to my colleagues at *Christian Weekly Newspapers* for bearing with me during the time the manuscript was being written (in holiday and spare time, I hasten to add!) and last but certainly not least to my wife Susan, who not only typed all the tape transcripts, the first draft and the final manuscript, but also had to put up with a virtual lodger instead of a husband for several weeks whilst I was eating, drinking, thinking – even dreaming – the London Emmanuel Choir.

I hope the result will convey something of the impact Edwin Shepherd made upon thousands of people in his lifetime; but more than that, the impact made by God upon the life of Edwin Shepherd.

JOHN CAPON
Redhill, October, 1971

CONTENTS

Chapter 1

TO BE WITH HIS LORD

Edwin Shepherd raised his hands expectantly. He looked up at the choir and smiled. This was his favourite Christmas carol of the 1970 festival and he was looking forward to conducting it. All the choir members had found their places and had their eyes on the conductor. He signalled to his wife Muriel at the piano to start the introduction and the tinkling notes of the piano sounded out through the packed Westminster Central Hall in London. Two downward runs and the choir were into this the last but one piece they were to sing on their own at the first performance of their annual Christmas Carol Festival.

'Christ was born in Bethlehem. Angel voices filled the air,
Peace on earth to everyone was their Christmas prayer.
Wise men came to Bethlehem with their gifts of gold and myrrh,
Glory to the Prince of Peace was their Christmas prayer.'

The tempo of the piece changed and the male voices were brought in to sing the melody with female voices accompanying.

'We can live this message . . .'

Suddenly, in mid beat, Edwin Shepherd paused. He seemed to smile and look down at his music. His elbows dropped and he started to fall forward over his music stand. For a split second, which to many people seemed like an eternity, everyone froze. Then Muriel Shepherd rushed forward from the piano and put her arm round him supporting him.

Other members of the choir came forward to help her and within seconds there was a group of people around the fallen conductor. As he was carried off the platform more than one choir member turned to his neighbour and remarked that they had just seen their choir leader go to be with his Lord.

* * *

The day had started normally enough for Edwin and Muriel Shepherd in their Banstead home. They were both looking forward to what was to be the 25th annual carol festival held by the London Emmanuel Choir since it was formed in 1945. Preparations had been going on for the festival for several months culminating in the final practice by the choir the previous Saturday, at the Westminster Chapel. Bookings for the five performances were well up to the normal level and as usual many thousands had been disappointed at not being able to get tickets for one or other of the performances. Wednesday, the first day of the four day festival, was preparation day and as was his custom, Edwin was to spend it in the Central Hall, together with his team of choir members, making the hall ready and finalising the various preparations.

It was a foggy day and the ever present threat of a power blackout as a result of the work to rule by members of the electricity industry added to the general gloom. Someone was to call at the house to drive Edwin up to London for the day's work. When the time for departure came and no car had arrived he became impatient with the delay for he was always a stickler for punctuality. When it began to look as though he would have to make his own way up to town, Muriel persuaded him to take their own car, leaving her to come up by train. They were just starting to pack the various bits and pieces into the car when the 'chauffeur' arrived with profuse apologies for the delay, and Edwin left home for the last time.

By the time he arrived at the Central Hall his team of helpers were already well on the way towards creating the familiar scene. Hundreds of coloured lights illuminated the Christmas tree, the balustrades, the Christmas star and the cross which had been features of the carol festivals for so many years. Each member of the team had his own appointed task and during the course of the day they went about them in their usual fashion with Edwin very much the foreman attending to a detail here, a small problem there, making a quick decision about that, having a brief consultation about something else and generally keeping the wheels turning smoothly and efficiently so that the hall would be ready by seven o'clock for the start of the first performance.

Looking back on the day in retrospect, many of those who were present in the team of helpers at the Central Hall have recalled remarks Edwin made to them that suggest he was not unaware of the significance of what was effectively to be his last day on earth. To several of those who had given up the day to assist in the preparations he had a special word of thanks, drawing attention to their long service with the choir and remarking, 'You've been in the choir for a long time and I've never thanked you for what you've done; I'd like to thank you now.' To some it seemed that he was tense and a little worried about the possibility of a power cut during the day, or even more important during the evening performance. (In fact there was a failure in the power supply during the afternoon from about two o'clock until half past four, during which the emergency lights were used.) Someone else remembers that he was concerned about problems which might arise from a meeting being held at the Central Hall the same night to protest at the plight of Soviet Jews. But others have remarked upon the fact that he did not seem to be so worried as in other years. Some little details worried him more than usual – the decorative lights on the organ were not to his liking and they all had to be taken off and remounted before he was satisfied.

When lunchtime came he took the choir members down to the newly-opened restaurant in the basement of the Central Hall and there had lunch with them. Those who were with him at table do not recall any unusual signs of strain or tiredness. When they returned from lunch they found that the power had been cut off and the premises were plunged into darkness, but the emergency power supply was brought into operation and when he was satisfied that this could provide sufficient light and power for the performance to go on even if there was a power cut during the evening he seemed quite happy.

The preparations continued during the afternoon; the microphones and spotlights were placed in position and connected to their control panels; the giant Christmas trees were decorated; all the miniature bulbs were tested; the other decorations were put into position and so on. There were one or two out of the ordinary jobs to see to. The special guest artiste for the carol festival was Betty Lou Mills, the Gospel singer from Eastbourne, and she was accompanied by a four piece ensemble whose instruments and amplification arrangements needed to be specially arranged. As was customary the missionary guests to the festival who had been notified to the Shepherds in advance were to receive floral bouquets during the performance. On this occasion they were to be brought in on a sleigh constructed by a handyman member of the choir and this had to be specially decorated for the occasion.

Meanwhile back in Banstead Muriel Shepherd was getting her things together before setting out in the car for the Central Hall. It was still very foggy in the South London area and she recalls she had one of her worst journeys up to town that afternoon. She arrived at the Central Hall, parked her car in the usual place a few minutes' walk from the main entrance and went upstairs to greet her husband. The power cut had just finished and the lights were back to normal. It was time to have tea.

'I think I'll change before tea today,' Edwin said to his wife. 'That'll give me plenty of time before the performance starts.'

Tea was a very happy and relaxed occasion, full of the fun and fellowship always associated with choir functions and anticipation of the evening's performance ahead of them.

Of those present only Edwin himself may have had just an inkling that this was to be their last meal together. Three years before when he was recovering from his earlier heart trouble, he had been talking to Colin Haughton, a member of Christian Recording Associates, a group of tape recording and electronics specialists who provide facilities for missionary organisations and other societies. In the course of their conversation the subject of death cropped up more than once.

'I think the Lord still has a few more years left for me,' said Edwin. 'If I had my wish it would be to go to glory while I was conducting the choir at the Central Hall.' Colin Haughton recalls that later in the conversation he again mentioned this desire, specifying the carol festival as being the one at which he would most like to go.

During the summer of 1969 when Edwin and Muriel were on holiday in Spain with their close friends John and Irene Weatherley, the same subject came up in conversation one day in Muriel's absence.

'I suppose this will be our last holiday together,' said Edwin.

'What do you mean?' asked John.

'I feel I've only got about 18 months to two years to go.'

John Weatherley, a family butcher at Caterham and a founder member of the choir, had also been feeling the strain and intimated his own desire to give up his choir responsibilities.

'John, stay with us,' said Edwin. 'It's 25 years next year and I'll tell you what we'll do. We'll have a spring festival, a dinner, an Albert Hall do and then I'll think about it too.'

Over a year later the three of them were talking together and this time Muriel was also with them.

'My time is drawing near,' said John.

'What do you mean?' said Muriel.

'My time for packing up the choir,' he said.

'You don't mean that, John,' she said. 'Does Edwin know?'

Edwin brushed it aside. 'He did mention it to me,' he said.

'Well, it doesn't seem as though you're going to now,' said John.

'Not until I can get somebody to take it over,' he said. 'I just can't walk out and leave it.'

'That's true,' John agreed, 'but in the last 18 months you haven't done much about it.'

'Oh yes I have,' he replied. 'I've had one or two people

in mind to take over but no one seems to be the right person.'

(In a letter he wrote to a correspondent early in 1969 he said: 'After my illness some time ago I was quite sure that something should be done to ensure the continued ministry of this grand body of men and women. The problem of course is to find a deputy or a successor. My particular task is so personal that it is quite a problem to envisage the person who will carry it on in the same spirit. I have looked around for a long time with this in mind, and have not felt led in any way to make any change up to the present time.')

As he sat down for tea at the Central Hall that afternoon he knew the 25th anniversary dinner of the choir and the thousand voice choir festival at the Albert Hall were both behind him. Did he have a premonition that this was to be his last carol festival?

After tea there were a hundred and one last minute jobs to be seen to. Members of the choir started arriving and went to their accustomed dressing rooms to change into choir dress. The team of 70 stewards started to assemble. The record stall in the foyer was set up and the hall started to come alive with a buzz of anticipation as the first members of the audience, a great number of whom had come many miles in coach parties and as individuals to attend, started filing into the auditorium. Thirty minutes before the start of the first performance he went to the stewards' room and prayed with them for God's blessing on their service.

From there he went to the choir, as was his custom, to lead the choir in a prayer of dedication for the evening's performance. One phrase he used in his prayer stood out in the minds of many choir members and took on special significance in view of the later events of the evening. He prayed that the Lord would take them all 'safely home' that night and as he passed one choir member on his way out he said quietly, 'and me too'.

Then while the choir members were filing on to the platform he went to the small room behind the stage where the guest artistes had gathered and prayed with them there. As the hands of the clock moved towards seven o'clock the platform party went to the bottom of the stairs leading up to the curtained entrance to the platform. Betty Lou Mills and her team of musicians were led on to the platform with Muriel Shepherd bringing up the rear. As she got to the top of the stairs, she stopped, turned and looked at her husband. On an impulse she stepped back down the stairs, kissed him and said, 'Have a lovely evening, dear.' It was the last thing she ever said to him.

The traditional round of applause greeted Edwin as he strode on to the platform to conduct what was to be the last performance of his life. He smilingly acknowledged his reception, turned immediately to the choir who were waiting in their places and led them in the familiar words of their introit:

'Sweet is the work my God, my King
To praise Thy name, give thanks and sing,
To show Thy love by morning light,
And talk of all Thy truth at night.'

He turned back to face the audience, welcomed them warmly, and invited them to join with the choir in singing the opening carol, 'As with gladness men of old, did the guiding star behold.' After prayer the programme proceeded with its customary variety of choir pieces interspersed with solos from Betty Lou Mills. Choir members looking back over the conduct of the festival can point to no specific indication that Edwin was not his normal self. One choir member recalls that he forgot his music and had to ask one of the girls in the choir to go out and fetch it for him. Another remembers that during one of the choir pieces with a tape-recorded orchestral backing he missed a beat, but to her surprise made no acknowledgement of having made a mistake as he normally did by pulling a face or smiling ruefully. Instead he carried on conducting with his head down.

Halfway through the programme came the traditional Carols by Candlelight led by the choir's piano accordion team during which Father Christmas, impersonated by one of the choir members, came on with the gaily decorated sleigh containing the floral bouquets for the missionaries present. As the sleigh was brought on to the platform, it got stuck on some power cables running across the floor. Edwin stepped forward to pull the sleigh clear of the cables. Muriel went over and tried to stop him, fearing the effort would be too much for him. But he got it free, and jokingly remarked to the audience, 'Sorry, ladies and gentlemen, the ice is a bit sticky up here tonight.'

After the Carols by Candlelight team had left the platform he had to negotiate two difficult American pieces which were being sung to a pre-recorded orchestral accompaniment. The tapes had only arrived a short time before the festival was due to take place and one of them had been recorded very poorly. It took him many hours of work on the tape to eliminate the surplus noise and extraneous material which marred the recording until he was at last satisfied it could be used. It was not easy to conduct the choir to such a pre-recorded accompaniment and Muriel Shepherd, sitting at the piano, recalls seeing him give a smile of relief when he came to the end of the difficult pieces.

Betty Lou Mills came forward to sing two more of her own compositions, after which the choir began the final three pieces they were to sing on their own. The lovely Minor Carol by Lila T. Gunter was followed by two new pieces the choir had not sung before, both by Edward Hughes. The first, Christmas Prayer, was a quiet lilting piece with a simple but attractive tune and charming words – Edwin had already declared it to be his favourite carol of the festival.

He took the choir through the opening lines. 'Christ was born in Bethlehem angel voices filled the air, Peace on earth to everyone . . .' and then the choir had to miss a beat coming in on the off beat with the words '. . . was their Christmas prayer.' The music was repeated for the next two lines and then the tempo and the harmony changed with the words 'We can live this message, we can make it true, if we live for others like Christ for me and you.' As the men took up the melody with 'We can live this message' Muriel looked up from the piano and saw that Edwin had stopped conducting. He was looking down at the music on his stand. His face which was wreathed in a beautiful smile seemed to be radiating a strange light, almost a glow. She saw his elbows begin to give and jumping up from the piano she rushed forward. Other members of the choir came forward too, but the choir continued singing, almost as though they had been switched on to automatic operation. One of the choir members came to the front to take the choir through the rest of the piece.

Nursing and medical staff from both the choir and the audience were among those who had come forward and together they got Edwin off the platform and behind the curtain shielding the entrance to the platform from the room behind. Muriel followed them out and stood to one side stunned. It had all happened so quickly. Perhaps 30 seconds had elapsed between the time he collapsed and the time they got him off the platform, but no more.

As they were attending to him she turned away and walked back on to the platform as the choir came to the end of Christmas Prayer. She went over to Betty Lou Mills, the soloist, and asked her if she would sing straight away, indicating to the choir that they would omit their next piece. Betty Lou Mills walked to the microphone.

'If you're anything like me,' she said quietly to the hushed congregation, 'at a time like this you want to pray. I suggest we all pray.' She paused for a moment to collect her thoughts, then she asked that the Lord would 'succour the mind of Edwin Shepherd and if possible restore him again. May Thy will be done.' Then she asked God to 'support Muriel Shepherd in a time of unknowables'. It was a wise and courageous decision to pray at that point. The tension eased visibly, and she started to sing.

As Betty Lou Mills came to the end of her second piece, someone said to Muriel, 'You'll finish now, of course.' But she was made of sterner stuff than that. She was convinced that if Edwin had recovered there and then he would have wanted the performance to go on, particularly because the next item involved a choir of deaf and dumb Christian young men and women who were going to perform with the choir. They were all waiting outside in the room behind the platform ready to come on. She went over to their leader, Albert Barritt, and suggested to him that they go on from the other side, she herself leading the way and starting the choir humming while the young people took their places. The choir sang the little piece 'Jesus good above all other' while the young people expressed the words in their own deaf and dumb language.

Meanwhile behind the curtain the ambulance men had arrived to take Edwin away. They lifted him gently on to a stretcher and took him down to the street by the quickest possible route. Two choir members went with him in the ambulance as it sped across Westminster Bridge and down Lambeth Palace Road, turning into St. Thomas's Hospital on the south bank of the River Thames. There he was quickly transferred to the resuscitation room just inside the entrance.

Back at the Central Hall the deaf and dumb young people finished their first piece and joined the choir in interpreting the hymn 'How great Thou art' in sign language. When they had finished Muriel turned to the audience and explained that her husband was seriously ill, apologised for cutting short the programme and invited them to join the choir in singing again the chorus from 'How great Thou art', after which the chief steward closed in prayer. Hardly had the great crescendo of noise from the last 'How great Thou art' and the magnificent final chord died away, than Muriel was speeding in John Weatherley's car to St. Thomas's Hospital.

When they arrived at the hospital they were shown into a room just near the resuscitation room where her husband lay. A doctor came out of the room and took Muriel gently by the arm. 'I'm sorry,' he said, 'but we can't offer you any hope. Your husband is desperately ill.'

Across the Thames at the Central Hall a prayer meeting was organised by the male members of the choir immediately at the close of the festival and the other choir members were standing around in groups unable to collect their thoughts after the tragic events earlier in the evening. Already the news had started to get around. The Rev. William White, minister of Banstead Baptist Church, where the Shepherd's were in membership, was told straight away and before the evening was out he had telephoned round to all the deacons of the church telling them of the situation and seeking their prayers.

Back at the hospital around midnight Muriel was allowed to see Edwin, who by this time had been transferred to the Intensive Care Unit. John Weatherley went in with her for a few brief moments, and stayed at the hospital until about one o'clock. The hospital staff offered Muriel a room with a bed for the night and he advised her to take it so that she would be on the spot if she were needed. Then he left, making her promise to call him if there was anything further he could do. Back in her room she stood looking out of the window at the traffic passing incessantly all through the night over Westminster Bridge and past County Hall. She thought, 'I wonder who all those people are in their cars going to and fro all night quite unaware of what's taking place in this hospital.'

Two Christian nurses came in to see her during the night making her ample cups of tea. As soon as they heard a Mr. Shepherd had been brought in they came to see her to check if it was 'the Mr. Shepherd of the London Emmanuel Choir.' One of them used to live in Banstead where the Shepherds lived and they were a great relief to Muriel, talking to her about her husband and about the choir, helping to take her mind off the tragic chain of events.

'I know God never makes a mistake,' she told them, 'and I'm just leaving it in His hands'. She could not yet bring herself to believe this was the end. She still believed a miracle could happen.

At seven o'clock in the morning, before it was light, she made her way from the hospital building to Victoria station, catching a train to Sutton and going from there by taxi to the strangely empty house from which she had said goodbye to her husband 24 hours earlier. Ann, her niece, who lived with them and worked in a local solicitor's office, took the day off and answered the telephone, which hardly stopped ringing all day.

As the day wore on and she sought to come to terms

with the situation, it never once occurred to her to call off the remaining concerts. John Weatherley had said to her the previous night at the hospital, 'I don't think you ought to go tomorrow night.' But she was emphatic that she should go on, that this was how Edwin would have wanted it. So as she tried to piece things together during the day the performance of the choir acted as a barrier preventing her grief overcoming her. She was conscious of the prayers of hundreds of people for her and was confident that they would carry her through, despite her own feeling of inadequacy. One of the many people who came to her assistance at that time was William White the Baptist minister at Banstead. He had planned to come to the festival on the Friday evening but offered to come on the Thursday and Saturday evenings as well to take over the job of announcing and linking the festival, even though it meant making alternative arrangements at short notice for his own mid-week Bible study meeting.

As the choir members gathered that Thursday evening for the start of the second performance there was an air of definite prayer and a feeling of sadness. Those who had the latest news about their leader passed it on with quiet voices and worried frowns. One reason for deciding to carry on with that night's performance so far as Muriel Shepherd was concerned was the well-being of the choir. She felt that they needed firm leading and a clear decision to continue. As the time came for the performance to start Mr. White went on to the platform after the choir and guests had assembled. Simply and quietly he told the audience exactly what had happened and introduced Muriel as conductor in her husband's absence, asking at her request that there should be no applause as she entered as was customary when Edwin went on to the platform.

Looking back she is quite sure that the only reason she was able to go through the remaining performances of the carol festival was the prevailing prayer of many hundreds of people for her and the spontaneous reaction of love and sympathy from the members of the choir which she experienced as she conducted them. Indeed on the Friday evening she had a quite remarkable experience when she felt a glow within herself which came out in her face. She is unable to put an adequate description to it but simply feels it was the time when God was very close to her. But not surprisingly she occasionally had difficulty in keeping her mind on what she was doing and several times she omitted to give the choir the signal to rise or sit.

When they came to the place in the programme where the choir was to sing Christmas Prayer she turned to the audience and said, 'We are now coming to the part in the programme where my husband collapsed last night and we are going to sing this as our Christmas prayer.'

After the performance on Thursday night John Weatherley took her to the hospital and together they went in to see Edwin. There had been no change from the situation earlier in the day and they did not stay long.

The Friday and Saturday night festivals were to be recorded for release subsequently as a long-playing record. Edwin had asked for this to be done following the success of the live recording at the Royal Albert Hall earlier in the year. This imposed an additional burden on Muriel, but she was sustained throughout this period by the fact that her husband was still alive and she refused to let herself think beyond that.

On Saturday two developments took her one stage nearer the moment she had been dreading. On Saturday morning she played over the Albert Hall recording which had just been issued. By one of those coincidences that seemed to many people to be the hand of Providence, the recording manager had asked Edwin to record a short verbal introduction to the festival to cover up some imperfection in the recording of the opening hymn. He came across on the record tired but cheerful and the sound of his voice so soon after the events of the previous days was too much for Muriel.

It was a sad day. She and her niece went out for a walk to try to keep their spirits up, but when she arrived at the Central Hall for the Saturday afternoon performance she knew it was going to be her most difficult yet. Not only that, but when she visited the hospital on Saturday the sister at St. Thomas's took her to one side and told her that

Edwin's chance of survival was nil. However she came through it all and the final performance on the Saturday evening was felt by many to be an eloquent tribute of praise and thanksgiving to God for raising up such a man as Edwin Shepherd and his equally talented wife.

On Sunday she tried to go to see Edwin in the afternoon, taking with her her younger sister Phyllis, who had been staying with her since the day after Edwin's collapse, and her brother-in-law Ted. But the fog again clamped down on the southern counties and they had to turn back. The same day she had a telephone call from her elder brother Eric Wood, who in earlier days had sung duets with Edwin and taken part in several of the choir's first festivals. He told her that during the day he had distinctly heard Edwin calling his name and he planned to come up to London to see him without further ado.

He arrived about lunch-time on Monday and together he and Muriel went to the hospital to see Edwin for the last time. He was lying there looking very much his old self. The colour had come back into his cheeks; the hardness, the tension, the strain had gone from his face and it is not surprising that at the sight of him Muriel broke down. She said to her brother, 'I want to say to him "The Lord hath given, the Lord hath taken away, blessed be the name of the Lord" but I don't want it to be of myself. Some people say the Lord gave me this and the Lord gave me that but I don't want it to be like that.' Eric prayed with them both and quoted one of the songs he used to sing as a duet with Edwin, 'O the wondrous love coming from above.'

As they left him and took off the gowns they had had to wear Eric asked the sister 'Will it be long?'

'No,' she said, 'It will be tonight.' Muriel knew then that she had seen her husband for the last time.

Edwin Shepherd passed away during the night. The hospital wisely did not disturb Muriel then but telephoned at seven o'clock on Tuesday morning to tell her the news she had been expecting. When she finally heard this confirmation she began to realise its implications. Since his collapse many things had shielded her from the full realisation of the loss she had suffered – the need for calmness and detachment in leading the choir and keeping faith with the thousands of people attending the carol festival, the faint ray of hope which she kept alive all the while he was still fighting for life, the love and sympathy and prayers of so many hundreds of people known and unknown. But in the cold light of a winter's morning she realised the full significance of her loneliness for the first time.

She made several telephone calls immediately to key members of the choir who had been acting as information points for other choir members and interested friends in order to preserve her own privacy. John Weatherley recalls that when he heard the news he had a feeling of great joy. All the while his friend had been in a coma he had been edgy and tense. When he heard that Edwin had gone he felt relieved and much happier. Like many people in the choir and amongst its supporters he had feared lest there might have been only a partial recovery that would have left Edwin a mere shadow of his former self.

The next hurdle to be overcome was an immediate one for the following day, Wednesday, the choir was to make a recording for the BBC radio programme *Sunday Half Hour* to be broadcast on the Sunday after Christmas. Fortunately the programme had been arranged well in advance and the choir was thoroughly prepared for the recording session, but as the members of the choir came together at the BBC Concert Hall, most, if not all were aware that their leader had died the previous day, and there was a solemnness and quietness about the proceedings that was quite unlike any normal choir function, when the chattering and laughter usually takes some time to subside. The programme's producer, the Rev. W. D. Kennedy Bell, sensed the air of despondency hanging over the choir and spoke to them before the recording session pointing out that had Edwin been alive the last thing he would have wanted was for the choir to give other than of its best at the recording.

Muriel Shepherd, who until that moment had really wondered how she could go through with the recording session, poured out her heart to the choir. 'You've got to help me and I've got to help you,' she said. And that's how it was.

Many choir members subsequently commented on the remarkable degree of sensitivity and appreciation by the choir of Muriel Shepherd's efforts on that occasion, so much so that at the end of the recording the producer came up to Muriel and said, 'If I had words to say of this lady I would say them but I haven't got any,' so he showed his admiration with a kiss.

On Sunday she conducted a section of the choir at the evening carol service at the Baptist Church in Banstead High Street, as previously arranged, and the following day Edwin's funeral service took place at the same church. It was to have been a private family affair, but in fact the small church was packed to the doors with choir members and other friends who came from many miles around to pay their final respects to their leader and friend. The service was conducted by the minister, William White, and Edwin's brother-in-law, Eric Wood. It included many of Edwin's favourite hymns and was a glorious service of triumph and hope.

In his address Eric Wood said that he felt sure Edwin's instruction to him would have been 'Don't speak about me; speak about my Saviour.' He never sought to draw attention to himself, he said, 'but my, how he loved Jesus.' His first impression of Edwin when he had entered their home in South East London over 40 years before was that he brought the fragrance of the love of Christ. He gave thanks to God for sending Edwin to their family and for calling him to the work of the London Emmanuel Choir, through which hundreds, if not thousands, had come to Christ. 'The secret of his life was his love for Jesus,' he said. 'Can you imagine Edwin Shepherd without Christ? I can't.' His life was like a smooth stone cast into a pond. The stone disappeared but the ripple it caused spread out in ever-widening circles long after the stone sank. So it was with Edwin's life.

He finished with a few lines found in someone's Bible which he thought fitted the situation perfectly:

'If I should die and leave you here awhile
Be not like others sore undone who keep

Long vigils by the silent dust and weep.
For my sake turn again to life and smile
Nerving thy heart and trembling hand to do
Something to comfort weaker hearts than thine.
Complete these dear unfinished tasks of mine
And I perchance may therein comfort you.'

Edwin was buried in the churchyard adjoining All Saint's Church just a few hundred yards from where the service was held. By one of those curious coincidences which were a feature of Edwin's life the church was the one in which Harold Pitstow, Master of the Bellringers at Westminster Abbey, worshipped, who was in the form above Edwin at Saffron Walden Grammar School.

It was somehow fitting that the choir had an engagement to fulfil on the evening of the day on which the funeral took place, the Bank of England carol service at Loughton. Muriel did not take part in this, so Robin Littler conducted the choir in her place.

With the dawning of the new year the trustees of the choir asked her to become its official conductor. She was ideally suited for the task. She had worked very closely with her husband in all aspects of the planning for and preparation of the choir's activities for over 25 years. A gifted musician and accompanist herself, she had amply demonstrated her ability to control and lead the choir during the remaining performances of the carol festival and no one else in the choir enjoyed the same confidence and respect as she.

The memorial service for Edwin Shepherd, held on January 20th, 1971, was led by William White, who had deputised for Edwin so ably at the carol festival, and many of those whose association with the choir had been longest and closest took part in a tribute to the memory of the choir's founder. The Westminster Central Hall was packed to capacity with those who had supported the choir throughout the years, among them Mrs. Mary Wilson, wife of the former Prime Minister, and at least one person who had flown over from the USA specially for the occasion.

The veteran evangelist Lindsay Glegg led the meeting in

a most eloquent prayer. Douglas White, who 26 years earlier had approached Edwin to form and take charge of a 200 voice choir to sing at the Jubilee Celebrations of the London Christian Endeavour Federation, the forerunner of the London Emmanuel Choir, paid a moving tribute to the man who had been not only a close personal friend but a colleague at Barclays Bank. As a staff manager at the bank he had been able to call for Edwin's personal records to be brought to him that morning from the vaults of the bank. He read out to the congregation one of the entries in the records: 'Mr. Shepherd has proved to be a truly loyal colleague with passionate qualities which have endeared him to both staff and customers, many of whom look upon him as a friend and one in whom they can confide'. Unlike so many Christians, he said, Edwin Shepherd lived out his Christian beliefs in his daily work. One of the choir members gave her testimony, speaking of the tremendous fellowship she had enjoyed with the choir and particularly of the help that Edwin Shepherd had been to her and all the choir members.

The Rev. Eric Wood, Edwin's brother-in-law, with whom he was so closely associated in the earlier part of his life, gave the closing address. He asked the question, what was the secret of Edwin's success?

'I think if Edwin could speak, he would say just simply this, "I believe God." He did not merely believe about God or in God, he believed God, and because he believed God he dedicated the whole of his life and talent that he might make known the excellencies of his Saviour whom he accepted in the Royal Albert Hall here in London those long years ago. He let Christ be not only the Saviour but the Lord of his life. He gave himself to the furtherance of the Gospel through the power which God had entrusted to him. We are thinking tonight about someone who was quite ordinary, but was made extraordinary by the power of the Holy Spirit.'

He went on to tell the story of a holiday he once had with Edwin when they went by car round the south coast of Devon and Cornwall and back along the north coast staying the final night at Lynton. 'We shared the driving and on the Saturday morning it was Edwin's turn to take over the wheel,' he said. 'We managed to make it up the hill out of Lynton and then up Countisbury and along the top road. Edwin was so disappointed because the mist was heavy on the land and we couldn't see the wonderful view across the Bristol Channel to Wales. Then we came to Porlock Hill, the steepest hill in the West Country, and we began to go down it. We negotiated the first hairpin bend and as we did so we came out of the cloud. There before our eyes was a simply stupendous sight. I was fascinated with it, but then I noticed that as we went down the slope with every yard we were gaining momentum. I saw the next hairpin bend coming up rather fast and I felt I had to say to Edwin "Don't you think you ought to put the brakes on?" "What do you mean?" he said, "I've got them on!"

'The last few miles of Edwin's life,' Eric Wood concluded, 'he had the brakes on, but he still went faster than many of us.'

The choir, which was conducted by Muriel Shepherd, sang many times during the service, including several of Edwin's special favourites, all of which summed up his own personal Christian beliefs: 'How sweet the name of Jesus sounds in a believer's ear', 'God is in every tomorrow', 'Let the whole world know', and a defiant, triumphant finale to the whole service, a repeat of the concluding piece from the Christmas carol festival, 'How Great Thou Art'. As choir and congregation joined in the singing of the last verse and chorus something of the rapturous joy of heaven filled their souls. A friend wrote to Muriel a day or so later: 'There surely has never been a memorial service like it. Not only was it a great tribute to Edwin but it brought real glory to God and a great uplift and blessing to the audience.'

Every choir member prayed that night for grace to follow humbly in the footsteps of the man of God whose example had been their inspiration for 25 years.

Chapter 2

THE FOUNDATIONS ARE LAID

Monday, December 9th, 1902, was an anxious day for all those at No. 9 Victoria Avenue, Saffron Walden. Three months old Teddy, the latest arrival in the family, was suffering from a severe attack of pneumonia and was not expected to live. His parents, Arthur and Alice Shepherd, called the vicar of St. Mary the Virgin Parish Church, the Rev. John Steel, to come to the house and baptise the young baby. The baptism duly took place but in fact Teddy made a complete recovery and by the following August was quite well enough for his parents to present him at the church.

Mr. and Mrs. Shepherd lived in a quiet side road on the southern fringes of the ancient market town of Saffron Walden and were well-known in the locality. Mr. Shepherd had been at one time a schoolmaster, but resources for education at the turn of the century were not very substantial and he became frustrated at the lack of progress he was making. He gave up teaching in due course and went into the tailoring profession, setting up his own tailor's business in the town. Still not satisfied he eventually joined the town council as a rate collector and combined this work with the secretaryship of the local hospital and any other secretarial work which came along.

Mrs. Shepherd was in the millinery business during her earlier years but soon after her marriage her eyesight deteriorated so seriously that for the rest of her life she was virtually blind, despite constant treatment, which included an abortive operation on her left eye. She had three children, Muriel, Charles and Edwin, or Teddy as he was known. Both she and her husband were loyal church people, Mr. Shepherd's father having been a local preacher at Stockport Chapel, Colchester, in earlier years. They attended the magnificent old parish church where Mr. Shepherd

Above: Mr. and Mrs. Arthur Shepherd.

Below: Edwin Shepherd (right) with his brother Charles and sister Muriel, 1908.

Above: The first eleven at King Edward's School, Saffron Walden, 1918. Edwin is standing on the extreme right. The two masters are (left) Mr. Morrison and (right) Mr. Parrack, the headmaster.

Below: Edwin in his early twenties.

Above: Edwin and Muriel on their wedding day, April 2nd, 1934.

Below: Wythes Road Baptist Church, Silvertown, where Edwin was lay pastor from 1937–1945.

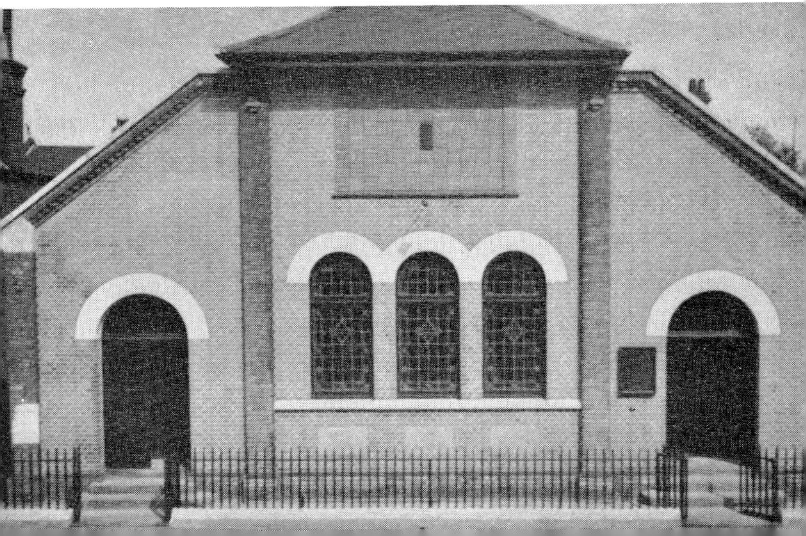

Above: The first group photograph of the London Endeavour Choir (as it then was), 1946. Strength: 102.

Below: One of the latest pictures of the London Emmanuel Choir, 1970. Strength: 149. Both photos taken in Westminster Central Hall.
Photo: Douglas F. Lawson, F.I.I.P., F.R.P.S., F.R.M.S.

was a Sunday school teacher for many years, being in charge of it for a short period. Each Sunday morning at breakfast the children would sit round the table quietly listening to their father reading a portion from the Bible.

They were a very musical family. Mr. Shepherd was a tenor in the church choir and Mrs. Shepherd, despite her blindness, used to play hymn tunes on the piano during the long summer evenings when the children had difficulty in getting to sleep. At other times neighbours used to open the windows of their houses to listen to the whole family singing round the piano. It was not surprising therefore that both Charles and Teddy joined the church choir very early on despite keen competition from other boys. The church was well patronised at that time, the congregation often filling the 1400-seat building, and there was no shortage of young voices for the choir.

Norman Preston, the well-known editor of Wisden's Cricketers' Almanack, was a member of the same choir, and recalls that Teddy had a very fine voice even at that age. It was no surprise when he was made top boy in the choir. No doubt Mr. Mahon, the church organist and a fine one at that, played a significant part in his musical development and appreciation. Teddy combined with his musical ability an early sense of humour and he was known locally as the one who was always getting into mischief.

He went to the Boys British School, a nonconformist institution, for his primary education as the Church of England school was in a down town area of Saffron Walden. In 1913 he graduated to King Edward VI's Grammar School in the town, a school which though small could trace its history back to its foundation in 1423 and boasted a royal charter, granted in 1549. His school reports for that period indicate that he had considerable potential in several subjects. By the time he reached the Upper Fourth he achieved and maintained top position in his form for several weeks and came first in the terminal examinations twice running.

He showed all-round ability not only in the class-room but on the sports-field, where he was particularly good at football and cricket, playing for the school at both games –

indeed he finished up as captain of the football team, when his headmaster noted he was 'very keen, sets a good example, improving rapidly'. His conduct at that time was described as 'generally good, must *always* make the most of his time', though whether this was a comment on his existing attitude or an exhortation for the future is not clear. Mr. Parrack, the headmaster, concluded his last report with the words, 'Has plenty of ability. With more determination will do very well indeed'.

What was probably his first spiritual experience of any significance took place while he was at King Edward VI's School. Together with Norman Preston, who was a form below him at school, he and a dozen or so others used to attend the Sunday afternoon Bible class held in the masters' common room by one of the teachers at the school, S. A. Morrison, later to become famous for his missionary activity in Africa. It was here that he had his first introduction to the robust, committed Christianity which was so different to the institutionalised, formal religion he had experienced up to that time.

Outside school hours his interests were mainly musical and sporting. On one or two occasions during the first world war when the town's football team was short of men he played for them at centre forward. He was a very fast runner, a neat dribbler and had a fine sense of balance. He was not quite so successful at cricket though he played regularly for the school. He was a slow left-arm bowler but batted right-handed. (Like many children at that time he was made to write right-handed though he was naturally left-handed.) New swimming baths were opened in the town in 1910 and he and his brother were among the first youngsters to take advantage of the novelty of so large an expanse of water in which to swim – the nearest coast was 50 miles away.

He did not learn to play the piano. His brother Charles had lessons but did not get on with them very well. Teddy's particular gift was composing doggerel to fit well-known hymn tunes. Some of these concerned the shortcomings of masters at school. Others more lyrical in nature were in the form of love sonnets to one or two girls who went to a very select ladies seminary in the town.

At the age of 17 he left home and went to London seeking employment. His first job was with the London Electrical Company. (He could scarcely have realised how significant those initials were to become later in his life.) He found lodgings in Highbury, north London, with a Mrs Caister, a Christian lady of Pentecostal persuasion who was to have a profound influence on his spiritual development. Edwin had not realised at this time the full significance of the Christian message. He had attended the church services as a member of the choir at Saffron Walden for nine years, and the experience had been valuable in that it provided a foundation both musically and spiritually for what was later to take place in his life. The Bible classes of S. A. Morrison took him a stage further along the pathway of faith, but it was not until he met Mrs. Caister that he realised the difference between someone who was merely a nominal church attender and someone who had experienced the reality of a personal confrontation with God and who enjoyed a personal relationship with Jesus Christ.

On more than one occasion Mrs. Caister demonstrated more eloquently than words could tell the quality and reality of her faith and her complete confidence in the effectiveness of believing prayer. There was one morning in particular when she had such a strong feeling that he was in some physical danger that she left what she was doing to get down on her knees and pray for him. When he came home that evening she asked, 'What danger have you been in today? I had a terrible burden of prayer for you at 11.15 this morning. I believe God heard and answered.'

Edwin was astonished, for he had indeed been in danger that morning. A request had come from the warehouse to the office where he worked for help in loading a heavy crate of cable on to a lorry. Together with several others he eagerly volunteered. They pushed the crate weighing several hundredweight on a small trolley up two planks on to the lorry. It was almost at the top when the trolley wheels slipped off the planks and the crate toppled off. Edwin was immediately below it trapped between the wall of the warehouse and the lorry. As he looked up he could see the crate about to fall on him and there seemed no escape. Miraculously, it seemed, the crate did not fall, but landed on the tail of the lorry, half on and half off. As it balanced there precariously everybody heaved a sigh of relief and congratulated Edwin on his fortunate escape. Edwin recalled with characteristic precision that the incident took place at 11.15, the time of Mrs. Caister's prayer.

In 1920 when he was 18 years old he took two momentous decisions which were to affect the whole of his future life. He left the electrical company where he had been working and applied to join Barclays Bank in London. His application was successful and he started the banking career which was to last all of 42 years and take him to a senior position in one of London's leading branches.

The other major decision affected his spiritual life. One day in September he was going down a street in Highbury and passed an open-air meeting. Some lively singing was taking place and he could not resist stopping to join in. One of the ladies associated with the group leading the open-air meeting came up to him and gave him a ticket inviting him to sing in a massed choir at the Royal Albert Hall the following month during a campaign conducted by Frederick and Arthur Wood, the famous brother evangelists who started the work of the Young Life Campaign. So it was that on October 4th, 1920, he paid his first visit to the Royal Albert Hall, which was to become the scene of so many of his later triumphs.

He was sitting in a seat behind the platform some way up just to the left of the organ. During the meeting the claims of Jesus Christ to be his personal Saviour and Lord were placed before him as never before, and when an appeal was made at the end of the meeting for those who wished to respond to the message to go forward he had no hesitation in leaving his seat and going to stand with others before the rostrum. The pianist at the meeting, the Rev. Baring Gould, singled him out from among the two hundred or so who had gone forward, and taking him to one side quietly led him to Christ. When he left the Albert Hall that night his heart was filled to overflowing with thankfulness to God at this new experience and he could hardly wait to share the news with his landlady. She too was overjoyed and together they knelt in her kitchen and gave thanks to God for Edwin's new found faith.

Early in his Christian life he was aware that God was directing his attention to the need to make restitution for some of the things he felt he had done wrong before he was converted, and with typical determination and thoroughness he sat down one evening and wrote a series of letters to those concerned testifying to his new found faith in Jesus Christ and seeking their forgiveness for any wrongs he had done them in past years.

He used to go home to Saffron Walden at weekends and, of course, his family soon knew of his conversion to Christ. Charles, his brother, was away from home in Colchester at that time, and Edwin used to read to his mother and take her to church on Sundays. But he was not satisfied with this as the only Christian witness he maintained in his own town, and he sought other ways in which he could make known his faith.

Despite the large measure of support for the established church in Saffron Walden there was a thriving non-conformist community dating from the early days of dissent in the sixteenth century. Congregational and Baptist churches were established in the town in the seventeenth and eighteenth centuries and no doubt influenced by the Pentecostal loyalties of his landlady it was to the Free Churches he turned for opportunities to witness. There was no Assemblies of God or Elim fellowship in the town at the time, but several of those of Pentecostal persuasion united together on Saturday afternoons for open-air services in the town's market place, in the shadow of St. Mary's Church. Joining first as a supporter of the work, giving his testimony from time to time, and graduating to the task of leading the singing at these meetings, he became a familiar figure in the market place.

As the number of people supporting the meetings grew they set up their headquarters in the local YMCA building in the High Street and started Saturday evening Gospel services there. Edwin used to conduct these meetings, and it was not long before his musical gifts began to come to the surface. He organised a band of musicians to accompany the singing with a variety of instruments, including a mouth organ, a harp and five violins, one of which he played himself. Visiting speakers would sometimes come for the weekend but Edwin did much of the preaching himself. At the end of the service there would often be an hour or so of hymn singing from *Redemption Songs*. These meetings were the forerunners of the recognised Assemblies of God fellowship established in Saffron Walden in 1928.

In 1922 Edwin's father died and this increased his sense of responsibility towards his now almost totally blind mother. His brother Charles returned from Colchester and lived at home with his mother for the next ten years until she died. It was not until Edwin's interests in London and his increasing commitment to Christian service there began to make fresh demands upon him that he reduced the number of visits to his home town.

By this time he was becoming quite well-known in Pentecostal circles for his musical and preaching abilities, so it was not surprising that in 1928 at the invitation of Ernest Rose, of the Assemblies of God, Edwin found himself booked to lead the singing at a three-week evangelistic mission at Boone Street Chapel, Lee, in South East London. He needed a place to stay for the duration of the mission and the people at Boone Street were able to make arrangements with a family well known in the district by virtue of the thriving bakery business which carried their name in the High Street. Their address was 10 Burnt Ash Hill, Lee, and the family's name was Wood.

* * *

Arthur and Florence Wood had not always lived in Lee. Originally Arthur Wood was from Norfolk, but he moved to Knockholt, then a small village in Kent, in 1898 where he met and married a local girl and set up home. He was a baker by trade and soon built up a successful business as the village baker. Married in 1904, they had four children, Arthur Eric, Muriel, Cecil John Philip and Phyllis. Arthur Wood was a pillar of the local Wesleyan Methodist Chapel and used to lead the singing at the Sunday services. His wife played the harmonium and so it was quite natural that the children should very early develop their musical gifts.

The two boys went to the village school about a mile and a half away from where they lived, but in those days a girl's education was considered less important so Muriel had to be content with a little old lady who gave lessons in the front room of her cottage while the obedient children stood demurely with their hands behind their backs.

It was from this lady that Muriel first learned the basic rudiments of playing the piano and such was her proficiency that though she only started learning when she was seven years old by the time she was nine she was able to deputise for her mother on the harmonium at the village chapel while her mother was looking after Cecil John. She had became familiar with the Methodist Hymn Book during earlier years when she used to find the hymn numbers for her father at the services. Sometimes the sheer joy of singing the lovely Methodist words and stirring tunes bought tears to her eyes as she sang.

When she was ten she went to a private school in Orpington where she boarded out with some Methodist friends. There her musical education continued with further lessons from a rather better qualified music teacher. At this stage she had a remarkable gift for sight-reading but was not able to improvise a single note.

After two years she went to the grammar school at Bromley cycling two and a half miles from her home to the station and then travelling the ten miles to Bromley by train. It was there that she made the greatest strides in her musical development taking the various musical examinations, grade by grade. Her brother Eric (always known by his second name as his father was Arthur) was developing a fine singing voice and soon started singing at concerts and services in the locality for which Muriel would accompany him on the piano.

In 1924 the family moved to Lee, where Arthur Wood again established his own bakery business. By this time Muriel had developed several other interests, and though she liked to go to church on Sundays, during the week she was much more interested in the cinema. They had not had any film-shows at Knockholt so she used to go to nearby Lewisham. The family attended Hither Green Methodist Church, but in retrospect Muriel does not feel the atmosphere there was very conducive to her spiritual growth. She recalls that her own attendance there was more for the social activity for which the church was known.

It is unlikely that the Wood family would ever have had any connections with the Boone Street Chapel people, for the sort of religion practised there was far removed from the correct, formal atmosphere of the Methodist Church, had not their youngest daughter Phyllis, who was never very healthy, developed tuberculosis in her leg. In those days the disease was much less easy to control and eradicate than in later years and after extensive treatment failed to have any appreciable effect Phyllis had to have a special support for her leg. One day when he was out calling on one of his customers Arthur Wood mentioned to them the illness which was crippling his youngest daughter and immediately they urged him to bring the child to their Pentecostal mission. 'We believe in divine healing at Boone Street Chapel,' they said.

The Wood family had never heard of any such thing and they discussed it among themselves. Grave doubts were expressed about the wisdom of visiting the rather despised mission hall but all arguments were silenced by Phyllis herself, who was only eight years old at the time, butting in and saying, 'I'll go and be healed'.

So Mr. and Mrs. Wood took Phyllis along to the chapel and during one of the services the leaders of the work placed their hands upon her and prayed for her healing. There was no instantaneous healing but her leg certainly improved noticeably within the succeeding months and in due time she recovered completely. Not surprisingly Mr. and Mrs. Wood started to attend the Pentecostal meetings at the chapel and enjoyed them immensely, but Muriel and Eric would have nothing to do with them – they felt that the simple mission hall was beneath them.

So it was that when the special crusade was to be held in 1927 and hospitality was requested for the man who was coming to lead the singing it was a natural response of thankfulness to God that led Mrs. Wood to offer her home.

* * *

Edwin Shepherd stood on the doorstep of No. 10 Burnt Ash Hill with a bunch of lilies of the valley in his hand. He knocked on the door and when it opened, presented the flowers, her favourite variety unknown to him, to Mrs. Wood, his face wreathed in smiles. Muriel happened to come home at the same time and was surprised to see the laughing young stranger. She had been expecting an elderly man to come. 'I didn't think young men were Christians, not keen Christians' she says, looking back, 'and I didn't think a Christian could laugh like he did, I just didn't understand it.'

Edwin stayed with the Woods for the duration of the crusade and impressed the whole family by his lively sense of humour and his transparent Christian faith, so much so that Muriel and Eric were persuaded against their better judgement to go to the final meeting of the crusade. Edwin as usual led the singing and also sang a solo. Eric was tremendously impressed by what he heard. It gave him a new understanding of the Christian message, as new to him as it had been to Edwin seven years before. Muriel was unimpressed, but when she went to bed that night she had a dream in which she saw herself as desperately wicked, and she could not understand how God could love her.

She continued in a state of considerable unhappiness and uncertainty until later that year when she went back to Knockholt to stay with an aunt for a weekend. They went to the Methodist Chapel for evening service together with a cousin of Muriel's and at the end of the service the preacher said, 'If any of you want to know more of God put up your hands.' Her cousin put up his hand and she thought to herself, 'Well, he wouldn't put up his hand unless he meant it', so she put up her hand as well. The preacher then asked those who had put their hands up to come to the vestry after the service and he knelt with them in prayer seeking God's blessing upon them. When she got to her feet Muriel did not feel any different, so she said to the preacher, 'I thought you felt different when you received the Holy Spirit and got converted.'

'Don't worry', he said 'feelings change.'

She was walking home along the village street with her aunt when God 'just filled my heart with his love'. It was something she was never to forget all her life. She knew she was saved, she knew what it was to be converted. A peace and a joy and a tremendous love came into her heart which she had not known before, so much so that when she returned to Lee the following day, her mother said when she opened the door, 'What ever has happened to you?'

Eric Wood had by this time developed into a fine singer. He had been having lessons with a professional singer in London and he had reached a position where he had to make up his mind as to whether he was going to become a full time professional singer himself or whether he should go into some other form of employment. He elected to stay in the bakery trade but in his spare time he and Muriel continued singing and playing at local concerts. However, it was not long before the new-found faith which Muriel and Eric now shared with Edwin bound them together in a closer bond of fellowship as they started singing the Gospel in mission halls and in special services around the area. Eric was a baritone and Edwin a tenor and they were ideally-suited duettists. Muriel was happy to play for them, her distaste for Sankey-type hymns now being a thing of the past.

'I realised I should often be called upon to play hymns and choruses without having the music before me,' she recalls, 'but I could not play a note without the music, not even the simple hymn tunes I had played from childhood. What was I to do? I prayed about my difficulty very specially one night. In my sleep a chorus came before my eyes and the next morning I went to the piano and played it. All my difficulty vanished. Ever since then I have been able to play hymns and choruses without music. This was indeed God undertaking in my life. I never cease to wonder at it and thank Him for enabling me to do this.'

Edwin became accepted in the Wood household as another member of the family, and he regularly used to spend weekends with them at Lee, going back to his digs and his job at the bank, where he had graduated to the position of cashier, during the week. But he did not neglect his own family at Saffron Walden. One Christmas he went back to spend the festive season with his people, and his brother Charles' girl friend, Doris, came round with her mother and some other relations thinking that Charles and Mrs. Shepherd were on their own. In fact with Edwin there they had a hilarious time finishing with a three-quarter mile trek to the station to see their guests off linking arms across the road and singing carols as they went.

Back at Lee meetings had started to be held in the Wood's home. The spacious lounge was cleared of furniture and turned into a little church for the services which were generally led by Eric and Edwin with Muriel at the piano. It was through these meetings that one of their most lasting friendships began – with John Weatherley. He worked at a butcher's shop in Keston and vividly recalls his first meeting with Edwin. He had come across to Lee on his motor bike to see Irene, a distant cousin of Muriel's, and was too shy to go in, so he stayed outside and sounded his hooter two or three times to indicate he was there. Edwin came running out to see what was happening and asked him why he didn't knock on the door and go in. John Weatherley did just that and as a result at one of the subsequent meetings held at the Wood's house, he too became a Christian.

Edwin's mother died in 1933 aged 66 and a year later Edwin and Muriel were married at South Lee Baptist Church on April 2nd, 1934. They had already decided to set up home in Banstead, Surrey, where some Methodist friends had told them of a fine plot of land for sale in Buckles Way, off the main London to Reigate road. Edwin's progress at the bank had been steady if not spectacular and he was able to erect a very substantial house on the piece of land which gave them magnificent views to the north – on a clear day they could see Windsor Castle, 21 miles away. John and Irene Weatherley, now their firm friends, came across from Caterham where they had set up home, to help Edwin and Muriel sort out the house and the very extensive garden.

Edwin continued to be active in singing and preaching in the London area – without Eric, who by this time had gone into training for the Baptist ministry. His voice had developed so well that he had started thinking seriously about becoming a full-time singer again, but one Good Friday afternoon at a Christian Endeavour meeting at Spurgeon's Tabernacle, Elephant and Castle, he was singing with Edwin when Mrs. Rowntree Clifford, of West Ham Central Mission, spoke to him.

'You ought to be in the Lord's work,' she said, 'We need you at West Ham.'

This made a great impression on Eric and shortly after that he left his job to become a worker at the West Ham mission, after which he underwent training for the Baptist ministry and became pastor of Upton Cross Baptist Church, one of the churches for which the West Ham Central Mission was responsible. Though he did not realise it at the time he still had a decisive part to play in the lives of his sister and brother-in-law.

The first development in which he played a significant role was the calling of Edwin Shepherd to the lay pastorate of Wythes Road Baptist Church, Silvertown, in London's dockland. The church was another of those under the control of the West Ham mission and had been without oversight for some time. There was only a handful of regular worshippers and the whole area was very run down. In the course of discussions at the mission Eric suggested his brother-in-law as a possible candidate for the job, but when he was first approached Edwin declined. Two further approaches were similarly turned down but on the fourth occasion Edwin and Muriel felt that this must be the clear call of God to them, so notwithstanding the 20 miles separating their home in Banstead and the church in Silvertown they accepted responsibility for the work there in the Autumn of 1937.

When they first arrived at the little church it was not a very prepossessing sight. Wythes Road was right in the heart of dockland on the narrow strip of land between the Royal Albert Docks and the River Thames, and the little church was dwarfed by the enormous cranes towering around the docks nearby, and the closely packed houses of the streets in the surrounding area were far removed from the spaciousness and light of Saffron Walden, Banstead and Knockholt to which they had been accustomed. Despite a fairly well-attended welcome meeting the early congregations at the services settled down at no more than a dozen, and for three months Edwin and Muriel had little to show for their labours. Then on the first Sunday of the New Year they had their first convert.

Naturally it was not long before music started to play an important part in the work at Silvertown. Edwin and Muriel, keenly aware of the value of music in the service of God, conceived the ambitious idea of producing J. H. Maunder's oratorio *Olivet to Calvary* in the church. They set about building up a choir from the slender resources they had at the mission. There was a Broadwood grand piano in the church and many hours were spent around that piano as they put members of the newly-formed choir through their paces. Few of them could read music and each part had to be gone through note by note to make sure it was known. But the enthusiasm aroused amongst the members of the small community was such that when they performed the oratorio on Palm Sunday, 1938, the church was packed to the doors and the event remained in people's minds for many years afterwards.

Edwin sought the help of John Weatherley in the work at Silvertown from the earliest days. He was reluctant to come at first having done no work of this sort before, but before long he was part of the team who piled into a car on Sunday mornings, drove the 20 miles to the London docks through the Blackwall Tunnel, down the East India Dock Road, across the entrance to the Royal Victoria Dock, down Silvertown Way and into the North Woolwich Road. The church was in the shadow of the large Tate and Lyle sugar refinery and most of those in the area worked either at the factory or in the docks.

Each Sunday John used to bring with him a prime cut off the joint from his butcher's shop at Caterham and a huge suet pudding which they cooked during the morning service and ate for lunch. During the afternoon Muriel led the Sunday school with the help of two teachers whilst Edwin and John went out on pastoral visits round the area. Then they had tea at the church and after the evening service they would all pile in the car again and come back to the genteel atmosphere of the Surrey suburbs.

Muriel used to go across to Silvertown on Wednesdays for the afternoon women's meeting which often used to attract 120 or more women from the surrounding area. Leaving Banstead early in the morning she would arrive at Silvertown at about eleven o'clock. The women's meeting did not start until 2.30 in the afternoon so she would spend the period in between visiting any who were in hospital or were too old to come out, together with anybody who had a particular need or problem.

Looking back over the passage of time that has elapsed since then she feels that both she and Edwin learnt a lot during those years because they were brought face to face with people and problems they had never experienced before. The East Enders did not take too kindly at first to this intrusion of people from a different social class and background, but once they saw that the motive behind their coming was one of love they were prepared to welcome them. Muriel found this work particularly enjoyable, as she had always wanted to be a minister's wife, but she was often taken into situations quite beyond her experience.

Edwin used to come down from the City on a Wednesday evening to conduct the mid-week Bible study at the church, after which they would both journey back to Banstead by car.

One day Edwin said to John Weatherley, 'Why don't you start a boy's club?'

'I don't think I could,' replied John.

'Oh yes you can,' said Edwin, 'I'll get you a book.' And he did.

The result was a very lively boys' club which met with great success, before being brought to an early end by the combined effects of the early bombing raids during the war and John's subsequent call-up for military service. (Edwin missed military service by a year, but he used to tell John when he came on leave that he always kept a bag packed ready just in case.)

They were all at Silvertown on Sunday, September 3rd, 1939, the day war was declared on Germany. During the morning service the first siren went. Barrage balloons started going up all round the church and people started to panic. Edwin had no alternative but to call the service off telling the congregation to hurry home or go to the shelters. Edwin and the rest of them waited a few minutes and then decided they had better make for home as well. They got as far as the Blackwall Tunnel and got caught up there in a gigantic traffic jam because the tunnel had to be closed during air raids. They sat there until the all-clear went and subsequently learned that the whole thing was a false alarm – it had been a British plane after all!

With the country at war difficulties in the work at Silvertown increased. Once bombing started in earnest it was likely that the docks would be among the first target areas, and for the next year all concerned lived in a constant state of uncertainty, but the work continued to flourish. The Sunday school reached between 50 and 60 children each week, the Sunday services were well attended and there was a tremendous sense of fellowship throughout the church. In view of the increased danger of travel in blacked out London, John Weatherley used to come across on Wednesday afternoons to Banstead to take Muriel over to Silvertown for the women's meeting and back again. They always tried to get back before night fell because the difficulties of driving with no street lamps and with heavily masked headlamps were considerable.

Despite the problems of those early war years there was no shortage of humour in the situation. On one occasion a sausage and mash dinner was arranged to celebrate the women's anniversary. Naturally the sausages were provided by John Weatherley – best quality pork sausages from his shop. However, either they had under-estimated the likely attendance or they had sadly misjudged the capacity of East Enders for pork sausages, because in no time at all they had all gone. Reserve supplies were obtained from a local butcher and by an act of gross misjustice

John found himself served with one of these inferior sausages instead of his own choice brand!

On another occasion when John and Edwin were in the car together driving towards Canning Town the air raid siren went, signalling an imminent bombing raid.

'We'd better keep going, John,' said Edwin.

They had just gone over London Bridge and were travelling along Whitechapel High Street. Suddenly John saw two bombs which seemed to be coming straight towards them. He was too petrified to do anything other than put his foot hard down on the accelerator, much to Edwin's alarm – he had not noticed the bombs at all. As it happened they passed safely over their heads and exploded a mile behind them.

The work at Silvertown came to a virtual stop following the first day of the London blitz, the so-called 'Black Saturday', September 7th, 1940. Edwin and Muriel Shepherd watched that night from their home in Banstead as wave upon wave of bombers burst through the meagre defences of the channel ports to release their bombs on and around the East End of London hour after hour. They saw the whole area lit up as though it was one gigantic bonfire. The bombardment went on long into the night

On Sunday morning Edwin telephoned John Weatherley.

'I think we ought to go up,' he said, 'just you and I'.

'All right,' said John, 'I'll be right over.'

They took the familiar route by car through West Croydon and up to the Blackwall Tunnel and as they neared the docks the terrible devastation became visible. Everywhere there were broken ruins of buildings and great acres of wasteland with piles of rubble and fires still burning from the night before. The tunnel itself was crowded with homeless people seeking shelter, but they eventually got through and made their way to the docks. They were initially prevented from entering by police who had sealed off the area, but Edwin talked persuasively to the officer in charge, explaining who he was, and the officer agreed to let them through.

They left the car there and made their way as best they could through what remained of the devastated streets. It was even worse than what they had seen on their way up – the remains of ships in the docks that had been sunk by the bombs, great floating hulks, some of them on end; cranes with their gibs mangled and broken; lorries and trailers burnt out and wrecked, railway lines twisted and torn with trucks scattered across the road running alongside.

When they eventually got to the church itself they were relieved to see that there did not appear to be very much damage to the building. Windows had been blown out and the brickwork at the back had been damaged but the building itself had escaped a direct hit, though the hall behind the church was in a much worse condition. All round the church rescue workers were busy combing through the debris in search of those who were still missing, bringing people out of the wreckage on stretchers, many near to death, some already there. In answer to their urgent enquiries Edwin and John learned that the survivors had all been evacuated to local schools as a temporary measure. With sinking hearts they retraced their steps to the car and set out on a tour of all the local schools seeking their flock. Eventually they found them in a school in East Ham and were immensely relieved to learn that nobody from the church fellowship had been lost during that particular raid.

Not surprisingly none of the evacuees had had anything to eat since the previous afternoon when the raid began. So Edwin and John got back into the car and went round looking for food. Fortunately the opening hours of shops in the East End were somewhat irregular and they were able to find a grocer's shop open at that time on a Sunday morning. John went in and asked the shopkeeper how many loaves of bread he had left.

'About ten or eleven, I think,' he replied.

'I'll take the lot,' said John, and he added to his purchases some hunks of cheese, butter, jam and pickles, pausing before he left to relieve the astonished grocer of his last remaining pints of milk.

Back into the car they went and off to the school at East Ham. They spread the food out on the bonnet of the car and organised an impromptu picnic. When all the food had gone Edwin made sure that all the people in his congregation were all right and then visited others in the area who had not been made homeless. It was six o'clock in the evening before he and John finally got home completely exhausted and very distressed at what they had seen.

The church was never quite the same after taking that dreadful hammering. Large numbers of the inhabitants of the area were evacuated immediately in case there was a recurrence of the crippling bombing raid. The Church of England building had been badly damaged and Edwin offered them the use of the Baptist church for their service, after which he held a short service on Sunday afternoons for those who were still in the area. All those who had been evacuated used to receive a monthly letter from the Shepherds telling them all that was going on and assuring them of their prayers. There was a short message from Edwin and items of news to keep them in touch.

As the war ran its course families started to drift back into the area, but they never restarted the morning service nor the boys' club. The women's work also came to a standstill for a time but as soon as it was possible Muriel went back to lead the weekly meeting as before.

In September, 1944, Muriel became seriously ill with hepatitis. Complications set in and she was rushed to hospital one Friday in October, the crisis coming on the following Sunday night. After an anxious few hours the danger subsided and she started a slow recovery. During this time Edwin continued the work at Silvertown in her absence, but it was obvious that they could not go on much longer. The doctors made it very clear that she would not be strong enough to return to that sort of work. She left hospital at Christmas, 1944, and through a lengthy period of convalescence was gradually nursed back to full health and strength.

Edwin and Muriel felt that in the circumstances they had no option but to inform the Cliffords at West Ham Central Mission that they could no longer continue the work at Silvertown. It had been in many ways a frustrating experience – seeds had been sown in the pre-war years for a real work of grace to be done in the hearts of the East

Enders, but the advent of war and the full fury of the German air-force on that September night took its toll, not only of the inhabitants of the area, but ultimately sapping the resources of those who had chosen to work there bringing some knowledge of the light and truth of Jesus Christ to an area of desperate need.

They were not to know that God was directing them to lay down one piece of service for him in order that they might take up another in a quite different sphere with ever-widening repercussions.

Chapter 3

A CHOIR IS BORN

At the beginning of 1945, Douglas White had a problem. He worked at a London bank so problems were nothing new to him, but this one was not concerned with his business life. In his spare time he was general secretary of the London Christian Endeavour Federation which linked together Christian Endeavour societies in London. It was founded in 1895, following the introduction of the Christian Endeavour movement from America eight years previously. For 50 years the London Federation had sought to promote the work of Christian Endeavour among young people in the London area and could look back upon several outstanding achievements in those 50 years, notably, the London Youth Evangelistic Campaign from 1929 to 1931, during the course of which no less than 325 meetings were held in 196 different parts of London with a total attendance of well over 300,000 people, resulting in more than ten thousand decision cards being signed and returned, and culminating in two great meetings in the Royal Albert Hall.

To mark the 50th anniversary of its foundation in 1945 special meetings had been arranged for Saturday September 15th, that year. Douglas White's problem lay in the fact that the BBC had asked him to arrange for a *Sunday Half-Hour* programme to be recorded in connection with the anniversary meetings and he felt that to lead the community singing on that occasion a choir would be needed. He and his executive committee had been discussing for some time the desirability of having a choir for the special meetings but the request from the BBC clinched the matter for him. There were no two ways about it. A choir had to be found. There were those on the committee who said it couldn't be done. 'We tried to get a choir together before the war,' they said. 'It wasn't any good then; surely it won't be possible now, not while we're still at war with Japan.' But the optimists on the committee prevailed and it was agreed.

The next question was: Who will lead it? It so happened that the incoming president of the London Federation for 1945 was the Rev. Eric Wood, at that time minister of Wood Grange Baptist Church. In the circumstances therefore it was hardly surprising that the name of Edwin Shepherd came up for discussion. Several other members of the committee already knew of Edwin's musical ability, and they felt there was no need to look further afield. When Edwin was approached he responded with enthusiasm. This was the sort of opportunity that he had long been seeking. He had always possessed the gift of getting people to sing whether in community hymn-singing or in smaller groups, and he grasped the opportunity presented to him by the jubilee celebrations with great eagerness. He was co-opted on to the executive committee and it was agreed that the choir should number some 200 voices.

One day soon after the decision had been made a young secretary at a London bank, Grace Alexander (now Jessup), who was on the executive committee of the London Christian Endeavour Federation was asked to go round to the pass-book counter where there was someone to see her. When she got there she found it was Edwin Shepherd. He laughed when he saw her, 'You don't know who I am do you?" he said.

'You're Mr. Shepherd,' Grace replied.

Edwin was taken aback, 'How did you know that?' he asked. Grace explained that she had heard him sing several times at Christian Endeavour meetings and other rallies.

'Douglas White sent me to see you to see if I could get you to do some work for me,' he said. So it was that Grace Alexander was enrolled as Edwin's unofficial secretary, little realising all that it would eventually involve her in during the greater part of the next 25 years as secretary of the London Emmanuel Choir. The first job was to write to all the Christian Endeavour societies in the London area asking for the names of members who might be interested in joining the choir. An advertisement was also placed in the *Christian Endeavour Times* appealing for volunteers to join the choir. The only qualification given was that those who volunteered must be familiar with Sankey's hymnbook. It is therefore rather surprising to find that all four pieces sung by the choir at the Jubilee Celebrations were from *Alexander's Hymns No. 3*, the famous hymn book compiled by Charles Alexander in connection with the Chapman-Alexander missions at the turn of the century.

These appeals for choir members produced a limited response and Edwin and others had to do quite a bit of personal work inviting friends and members of their churches to join with them in this venture. Eventually the choir was complete and the business of rehearsing got under way. Area rehearsals were held as the choir had been drawn from such a wide area. Muriel attended the practices as accompanist and so was born for the first time in a major way the husband and wife partnership which was to have such an influence on evangelical music for the next 25 years.

The jubilee celebrations commenced with an afternoon meeting at Westminster Chapel in London on the theme 'Endeavour's Greatness, the Voice of the Past'. The London Endeavour Choir, as it was then called, sang two pieces, the first of which could be said to sum up all that the choir has sought to do in the years since.

> 'All hail to Thee Emmanuel, we cast our crowns before Thee;
> Let every heart obey Thy will and every voice adore Thee.
> In praise to Thee our Saviour King,
> The vibrant chords of heaven ring,
> And echo back the mighty strain:
> All hail, Emmanuel!
>
> Hail to the King we love so well, Hail, Emmanuel!
> Glory and honour and majesty, wisdom and power be unto Thee,
> Now and evermore!
> Hail to the King we love so well, Hail, Emmanuel!
> King of Kings and Lord of lords,
> All hail, Emmanuel!'

It is interesting to note that the fifth word the choir ever sang together was the word Emmanuel. They could not at that time have foreseen their subsequent change of name which was to utilise that word and give it a whole new significance for generations of Christians.

The second piece they sang was 'Oh the deep deep love of Jesus'. At 5.30 p.m. after a break for tea the BBC recording for *Sunday Half-Hour* took place. Douglas White introduced the programme, Eric Wood sang a solo and the choir led the community hymn-singing. At the evening rally, under the title 'Endeavour's Opportunity, the Voice of the Future', Eric Wood took the chair and the speaker was the Rev. W. G. Channon. The choir sang two more pieces from *Alexanders No. 3*, 'Far beyond all human comprehension' and 'Awake, awake and sing the blessed story'. It was generally agreed that the meetings were a great success, but there was no doubt who had stolen the limelight – the London Endeavour Choir.

All the preparation and practice had been aimed at producing a once-only choir that would serve its purpose at the jubilee celebrations and then disband, but even before the meetings were over there were widespread demands that the choir should not be allowed to break up. Edwin Shepherd responded to this fresh challenge with immediate enthusiasm. The performance of the choir, raw and ragged though it may seem in retrospect, had confirmed his own feelings concerning the potential blessing that could come from a group of truly dedicated and disciplined Christians singing the praises of God. He immediately set about reconstituting the choir and wrote to all those who had taken part in the jubilee celebrations seeking their support.

Many of those who had been prepared to sing at the two London meetings were quite reasonably not disposed to make any further commitment in the way of a continuing choir. But out of the 200 original members around 90 signified their willingess to meet together and form a permanent choir, to be of service not only to the Christian Endeavour movement in London but also in wider spheres of ministry.

The first need was to get the choir trained in part singing

and voice control. Many of those who joined in the early days could not read a note of music and at the early practice sessions it was often necessary for each part to be dealt with separately, Muriel banging out their notes on the piano for them to follow time and time again until they got them right. The early practices were held in the Field Lane Institution, formerly a ragged school, on the top floor of the building, reached by what seemed to some of the older choir members a never-ending flight of stone steps. The premises left a lot to be desired in other respects, too. On one occasion during a particularly strenuous piece of conducting Edwin trod heavily on a rotten floorboard and his foot went right through the platform.

An early problem encountered by the Shepherds was the provision of music. For one thing it was no easy job to find any new music at that time, as the war was only just over and paper was severely rationed. There was also the problem of providing 90 copies of whatever pieces of music might be selected. *Alexanders No. 3* was the staple diet of the choir in early years, providing as it did a considerable number of tuneful melodies with good words and easy-to-follow harmonies, together with a book called *Hymns from Lambeth*. But as fresh music, both British and American, began to be available it was added to the music library. All the music was the property of the choir, purchased by choir funds. It was handed out at each practice and collected again afterwards. Each member of the choir paid a 4/- enrolment subscription to help finance the purchase of new music and other expenses.

At that time they were not practising specifically for any service or event in the foreseeable future, but rather Edwin was seeking to train the choir in the basic rudiments of singing so that when the occasion arose they could give a good account of themselves. Towards the middle of 1946 when the choir had been practising for some months Edwin felt sufficiently confident to make arrangements for a Christmas carol service later that year. Greatly daring he booked the Memorial Hall in Farringdon Street for one night, December 11th. There was nothing particularly outstanding about the programme. Three traditional carols were sung by the audience and the choir performed nine Christmas pieces ending with 'Lift up your heads' from the Messiah. Alfred Godbold and Doreen Garlick were the two soloists and the Christmas message was given by A. Lindsay Glegg, who had been familiar with the singing abilities of Edwin Shepherd and Eric Wood in pre-war days.

Something of Edwin's showmanship, which was to mark all the subsequent festivals and concerts, was present at that first carol service. Three Father Christmases patrolled the area outside selling programmes, price 6d. each. Such self-advertisement was unnecessary, however; the hall was packed out before they started. The choir appeared in their first 'uniforms', dark suits and ties for the men, white blouses and ordinary skirts for the women. They sang in very cramped surroundings, some of the men having to sit on narrow planks balanced precariously on rather insecure supports. Lindsay Glegg had to deliver his message from the platform steps as there was no other room available. No charge was made for admission at this first concert nor were any tickets issued, but a note in the programme records that a silver collection was taken up during the singing of the last carol.

Such was the response to this first public appearance of the re-formed London Endeavour Choir that during the next twelve months many calls were made on the choir for evangelistic and convention singing, including various Christian Endeavour conventions, a united campaign at the Royal Albert Hall, Bible Day at Westminster Central Hall, the World's Evangelical Alliance meeting at Caxton Hall, the Sentinel's meeting at Livingstone Hall, and an evangelistic campaign at Charlton, as well as visits to Brighton, Dorking, Guildford, Ashford, Epsom and Whyteleafe. By this time the choir rehearsals had moved from the Field Lane Institution to Bermondsey Central Hall.

Greatly encouraged by the public response to the choir, Edwin and Muriel determined to go one better for their Christmas Carol Festival in 1947, and with some trepidation they booked the Westminster Central Hall, seating 2,500, for Saturday, December 13th. They need not have worried; the hall was full, this time to hear a more substantial selection of Christmas melodies than the previous year. For some reason the words of all the carols were reprinted in the programme – could it have been that at that time the enunciation of the words by the choir left something to be desired? Lindsay Glegg was the guest speaker once more and among the soloists was the familiar name of Eric Wood.

'The tide of music's golden sea flowing towards eternity' was the quotation on the cover of the choir's next major public function some four months later, a Fantasia of Gospel Music, again at Westminster Central Hall. Lindsay Glegg's son Donal gave a series of parables linking the choir pieces, readings and solos.

Such was the increasing response to the choir that the 1948 Carol Festival had two performances, 3 p.m. and 7 p.m. at the Central Hall, Westminster, the platform and balustrades of which were festooned with coloured lights and other festive decorations. The choir was having a problem about the vexed question of applause at the festivals, for underneath the announcement in the programme concerning the names of those who were to give the closing message there was a note asking the audience if they would 'kindly refrain from applause here'!

Something of the potential ministry of the choir in the future was dawning upon the Shepherds because included in the programme for the 1948 festival was a postcard ready-addressed to the choir at 20 Buckles Way, Banstead, (the present address, 34 Buckles Way, was the result of renumbering the road, not a change of house) inviting people to give their names and addresses if they would like 'early information of future events' to be sent to them. In this way they hoped to build up a mailing list of people upon whom they could count for regular support.

In 1949 instead of a spring meeting the choir provided an 'Appreciation of Harvest' on October 8th at the Central Hall. 'The day approaches when this great London shall be girt with praise, and every beating heart in her shall raise a song to Him whom heaven and earth obeys,' was the verse Edwin chose to explain the purpose of the meeting. He had the first of many colourful ideas for livening up his festivals on this occasion. During the singing of the opening hymn people dressed to represent twelve different countries entered the hall from all sides carrying harvest produce from their country and placing it on a display mounted on a special platform extension.

At the carol festival that year Edwin went one better. He managed to persuade Gordon Wooderson, captain of the 88th London Company of the Boys' Brigade attached to Ramsden Road Baptist Church, Balham, to bring his silver band to the Central Hall to provide an accompaniment for some community carol-singing. Much to the delight of the audience he persuaded them to dress up to represent old fashioned waits of a hundred years ago. Special scenery representing an old-fashioned street scene, painted by Donal Glegg, adorned the balustrades either side of the Central Hall platform which was again extended to enable the band to stand in a semi-circle around Gordon Wooderson, who conducted them and introduced the carols. The music might have been less than perfect but the audience loved it.

The choir uniform had been modified a little by this time. Experience at numerous meetings since the foundation of the choir had quickly convinced Muriel Shepherd of both the impracticability and indignity often occasioned by wearing skirts of varying lengths on a high platform. She deduced that the only satisfactory answer was for the choir ladies to wear full-length skirts. The small black bows they wore with their white blouses had been emulated by the men who had dispensed with their ties and instead wore smart wing collars and black bow ties. As clothes were still severely rationed in the immediate post-war years several of them used to wear paper collars and waiters' white fronts from Woolworths, for which clothing coupons were not required, cleaning them up after use and making them last two or three times.

On the Sunday immediately following the carol festival the choir took part in its second *Sunday Half-Hour* broadcast for the BBC. This time they sang two pieces on their own, 'O leave your sheep' and 'Who is He?' The programme came from Wood Grange Baptist Church where Eric Wood was the minister.

Ever seeking for new means of reaching out with the Gospel through the ministry of the choir, Edwin conceived the idea of a choir holiday, and decided on Scarborough as the testing ground for this experiment. It was typical of his thorough planning that he started making this known well over a year before it took place encouraging those who followed the choir to consider making Scarborough their holiday resort that year and lend their support to the choir's efforts.

By this time the choir numbered around 130 and to ease administrative problems each member was given a number by which they were known and referred to in all documentation. In order to cope with the increasing size of the music library choir members were made responsible for keeping their own complete set, rather than being issued with each piece as required and returning it to the library after use. Each piece in the choir's repertoire was numbered and choir members were given a folder in which they kept all the music. For each practice or engagement they simply brought along the pieces that were required for that occasion. It was a standing joke in earlier years that the choir members needed to take the whole of their music to each engagement in order to sing perhaps a couple of pieces. A humourous skit along these lines was performed at one of the Christmas parties which were a feature of the choir's early years.

On Good Friday, April 7th, 1950, Edwin was inducted as President of the London Christian Endeavour Federation at the 55th annual convention at Bloomsbury Central Baptist Church. He took as his theme for the year 'Unconditional Surrender' and in his message to the Federation he wrote:

'My call to you for the coming year is not for a more intensive application to the tasks in hand, but for a complete and unconditional surrender to Jesus Christ himself. Make your relationship to him one of love, trust and complete loyalty. We have submitted too long to the spirit of defeatism. Let us advance to the attack and welcome the revival that is surely on its way by giving ourselves unconditionally to the high endeavour of our discipleship. Unconditional surrender to Jesus Christ is a sure pathway to blessing.'

During his presidential year he visited various parts of London with the choir, giving a special programme entitled 'Music with a Meaning'. Among other places they visited Croydon, Bromley, Harrow, Ealing, Tooting, Forest Gate, Islington, Woodford, Peckham, Hackney and Chingford.

Three weeks after his induction Edwin led the choir in the first of the spring festivals at the Central Hall entitled 'The Spring Awakening'. Another of his favourite verses adorned the programme:

'How wonderful if the spring should break
And the latter rain should fall,
How wonderful if earth should wake
In answer to God's call.'

Later in the year, from July 22nd to 26th, the eleventh Christian Endeavour World Convention was held in London and it was only natural that the London Endeavour Choir should lead the festival of praise which opened the proceedings on the Saturday evening. The pieces sung by the choir on that occasion are an apt illustration of the catholicity of their musical tastes at that time. Among the composers or arrangers represented were Handel, Sir Hugh Roberton, Gordon Jacob, Eric Thiman, J. B. Stainer and Norman Clayton.

On September 2nd the choir set off for their first ever holiday together at Scarborough, on the Yorkshire coast. Every evening they provided a full programme of Gospel music at the Scarborough Central Hall and once the word got around the hall was packed to the doors, rivalling in popularity many of the beach shows and pavilion entertainments on the sea front. Lindsay Glegg was the guest speaker for the holiday and before he was called back to London because of his wife's illness he went with the choir on a coach trip to Flamborough Head. On their way through the Yorkshire town of Filey they passed by the recently opened Butlin's Holiday Camp which occupied a commanding site overlooking the sea.

'My, wouldn't that be a fine place to have a Christian convention', he was heard to remark, and the first seeds of an idea were sown which eventually led to the establishment of the Filey Christian Holiday Crusade five years later.

The carol festival that year dispensed with a special speaker. Instead the Rev. and Mrs. C. W. Slemming presented the Christmas story through a meticulous re-creation of the familiar events of the Bible narrative using authentic biblical costumes.

A year later, always seeking for something new and unusual to enliven the carol festival Edwin Shepherd invited Derek Elphinstone, an actor who was a member at Westminster Chapel in London, to produce a short play. He responded with 'Born to be King', a fitting finale to a programme of Christmas music which ranged from 'The First Nowell' to an old French melody arranged by Gustav Holst. The extent of festive decorations at the carol festivals each year increased. A star and a cross illuminated with miniature light bulbs were added to the existing coloured lights, and plentiful displays of holly, ivy, yew and evergreens added to the seasonal atmosphere, together with two 15-foot Christmas trees provided by one of the choir members, a farmer from Crockenhill. One year it was decided to whitewash them to make them look snow-covered, but while one of them was being fixed in position it somehow got out of control and crashed forward on to the choir seats, covering them with flakes of whitewash.

Membership of the choir had now reached 150 and Edwin Shepherd felt that this was the size it should remain. A waiting list was instituted, therefore, and ever since there have generally been more people wishing to join the choir than there are places vacant. Anyone wanting to join the choir had to complete an application form, after which they were given a voice test, usually held before choir rehearsal. They were asked to sing some scales, pitch notes accurately, sing the top and bottom notes of their range and generally satisfy Edwin and Muriel Shepherd of their basic musical ability.

But musical ability was not the only, or necessarily the most important, criterion by which suitability for choir membership was judged. One of the first questions Edwin asked any intending member was, 'Are you a Christian?' He was convinced that first and foremost every choir member must be sure of their own personal faith in Jesus Christ as Saviour and Lord. He asked them why they wanted to join the choir and was always interested to know about a person's background or special circumstances. One choir member recalls that when she had her voice test the waiting list for sopranos was two years, but because she explained to him that she was feeling spiritually very low at that time following a difficult experience, he invited her to join the practices within a fortnight of her voice test.

Generally the choir was always short of male singers, so tenors and basses, especially the former, could usually expect an easier passage at the voice test, though not often as easy as one member of the choir who claims that when he presented himself in the little room, Edwin said to him 'Let's hear your top and bottom notes and you're in'!

In the earlier years of the choir a husband or wife were often accepted for membership of the choir because their partner had joined; Edwin did not like to separate a couple if he could help it. Once a person had been accepted in principle for membership of the choir he was either put on the waiting list or invited to 'sit in' at the practices. As there were only 150 sets of music he had to wait until a vacancy occurred within his section. The folder of music was then handed over at a short ceremony at one of the practices, he paid his subscription, and was duly enrolled as a member of the choir.

The men provide their own uniform. The ladies have their own skirts made – or make them themselves – from material purchased in bulk by Muriel Shepherd. Blouses, too, are ordered in large quantities to enable choir members to buy their own at reduced prices. The scarlet capes introduced in 1953 remain the property of the choir.

Every member has to sign the covenant which commits him to 'aim at attending 100 per cent of practices.' If his attendance drops below 75 per cent he is required to tender his resignation. He also promises to 'be punctual at all times, and if through illness or any other circumstance I am absent from practices for longer than two weeks will advise the cause of my absence by writing or telephone'. He undertakes to be present at all the spring and carol festivals unless prevented by illness or business commitments and promises to fulfil his choir engagements, faithfully notifying the secretary by postcard or telephone if he is prevented from attending.

'I will take care of all music and the New Testament issued to me and will return these in good order when leaving the choir. I undertake to replace any lost pieces at my own cost and will not use music issued to the choir for occasions other than those arranged by the conductor. I will conform to the accepted choir dress and undertake to wear it to choir engagements only.' And these are not mere words. At each weekly practice choir members are expected to sign on and a register is kept and inspected each year.

Practices in the early days were very much more heartbreaking and musically unrewarding than in later years. Because many of the early choir members were unable to read music they had to be taught their parts almost individually note by note, thus involving long hours of practice round the piano going over and over each section again. Once this nucleus of singers had been built up, able to cope with reading a piece of music at fairly short notice, the practices became much less a matter of drudgery and more a question of interpretation. Each practice began with the words 'Before we start . . .', which were the prelude to a short devotional message from Edwin Shepherd followed by a time of prayer. Thus the whole practice was set within the context of an act of worship and service to God.

Edwin spent a long time selecting pieces of music from the vast number he received gratuitously through the post from music publishers and other interested friends. He looked first for those with words that were strong and carried a message. Then he asked Muriel to play over the tune of such a piece and if the music matched the quality of the words he noted it down on his list. It had to be unhackneyed and fresh, tuneful and rhythmic to pass the test. After further examination and trial he made a decision one way or the other. If it was to be included in the choir's repertoire he needed to order sufficient copies for each member. If, as was often the case, the music came from America this could mean a delay of anything up to three months before the copies came to hand for the choir to try out the piece. Once the music arrived it was distributed at choir practice and the first rehearsal began.

Edwin spent a lot of time on each piece before the first rehearsal, going through it phrase by phrase and line by line, seeking to get the feel of the piece and mastering it completely himself so that when the choir came to sing it they could take a good lead from him. Sometimes the music or the words were particularly difficult and required additional explanation. He went to great lengths to meet the choir members in this, on several occasions typing out a whole page of explanation of the spiritual significance behind words which might seem rather obscure, so that when they sang them they would be able to do so from the heart.

He tended to leave the musical interpretation until the choir had mastered the basic melody and harmonies, but every night at home he would 'go over his music' sifting through it and studying every piece to assess how best he could interpret it. Sometimes at choir practice he acted out the character portrayed in the piece – an old coloured man for a negro spiritual, for instance – and in this way he was able to put across to the choir how he wanted them to sing it.

Though choir practices were serious times of intense concentration, his natural ebullience and good humour were rarely far from the surface, and he constantly interpolated injunctions and exhortations with jokes, anecdotes and cross talk with Muriel at the piano. He was severe with choir members who did not pay attention or who strayed from the paths of his direction, but there was never any rancour in his rebuke. He was giving of his best and he expected the choir members to do likewise.

In the summer of 1952 a party of 65 choir members went to Torquay, on the South Devon coast, for a fortnight's holiday, singing each evening at Upton Vale Baptist

Church. Such was the attraction of the choir that on occasions people started queuing outside the church three hours or more before the doors opened. The stewards were often put to great difficulties trying to fit more people into a building already filled to capacity. People used to sit on the stairs and window ledges and even on the floor in order to hear the choir. One small boy somehow managed to get a seat right at the front of the church every night. On the last night of the choir's visit he went to the church straight from school and missed his tea in order to make sure of his seat close to Muriel Shepherd at the piano.

The outstanding event of the fortnight occurred late one evening towards the end of the holiday. With a typical sense of the dramatic Edwin Shepherd hired two boats to sail into the harbour with the choir on board, there to anchor and provide an open air evening concert. At one stage it looked as though the boat trip might have to be cancelled because the sea was rough and the skies overcast, but as the day wore on the skies cleared and the sea grew calm. So it was that as the holiday makers of Torquay were taking a late stroll along the promenade they became conscious of the sound of Gospel music wafting across the waters. Spotlights from the shore picked out the choir, immaculate as always in their uniform, and many stayed to listen who would never have thought of entering the church where the other meetings had taken place.

The climax to the evening came when the boats started to move away from the shore and the choir commenced their final piece. At a word from their conductor each choir member lit a torch and as the boats, outlined against the darkness by the lights from the choir's torches, sailed gently away from the listening crowds the poignant words of Henry Francis Lyte's famous hymn 'Abide with me, fast falls the eventide' carried over the waters, gradually fading away as the boats receded into the distance. It was a memorable and an unashamedly emotional end to an amazing fortnight of praise and testimony in song.

Chapter 4

O COME, EMMANUEL

Most people in London got up earlier than usual on the morning of June 2nd, 1953. It was the Coronation day of the young Queen Elizabeth II who had succeeded to the throne with her consort, Philip, the previous year on the death of her father, King George VI. Thousands of school children and older people in the London area and the Home Counties made their way at the crack of dawn to the centre of London to line the processional route from Buckingham Palace to Westminster Abbey and back. The ceremony itself was full of religious significance with the Archbishops of Canterbury and York playing a leading role in the service and the presentation of the Coronation Bible, described as 'the most valuable thing this world affords'. But Edwin Shepherd, with characteristic flair, decided that there should be a more specifically evangelical contribution to the celebrations in London.

When the date of the Coronation was first announced the previous year he immediately telephoned the manager of the Westminster Central Hall to book the premises for the following evening in order to hold a special Coronation Festival in honour of the great day. For such an occasion some ceremonial music was obviously in order and he engaged the services of two trumpeters to provide a fanfare to introduce the programme and to join with the organ in Purcell's *Trumpet Tune and Air* and Jeremiah Clarke's *Trumpet Voluntary*. The choir sang a selection of suitably majestic and regal pieces, plus a few less heavy ones like, 'I'm glad to know he's mine' and 'Jesus paid it all'. The veteran Methodist leader, Dr. W. E. Sangster, was the main speaker, preaching from his 'home' pulpit.

Two special features which marked out this festival as different and long to be remembered were the special souvenir programme costing 2s.6d. which contained full colour illustrations of the crown jewels and other regalia used during the Coronation service, and the appearance of the choir ladies wearing for the first time scarlet capes, which drew a spontaneous burst of applause as they entered. There was a severely practical as well as a ceremonial reason for the capes. The choir had been called upon to sing and wait around in too many poorly heated halls and draughty corridors and the thin blouses which they wore as uniform provided little or no protection against such discomfort. The capes brought a vivid flash of colour to the platform which has remained one of the choir's best known trade marks ever since.

Typical of Edwin Shepherd's concern for the smallest detail in anything he did was the instruction added at the foot of the information sheet issued to each choir member in advance of the Coronation festival: 'Members of the choir entering through Door L will carry their music in the left hand and those entering through Door I in the right hand. Music will be transferred to the front as you turn to the front.'

Two days before the Coronation the choir had again been on duty, this time at the Royal Albert Hall for a United Service of Prayer and Dedication on the eve of the Coronation, held under the auspices of the World's Evangelical Alliance. The choir sang three pieces during the musical programme which preceded the main meetings, three pieces during the service itself and one piece at its conclusion. Among those taking part were the Archbishop of Sydney, the Bishop of Liverpool, the Moderator of the Free Church Federal Council, the General of the Salvation Army and, again, Dr. W. E. Sangster, under the chairmanship of Lieut.-General Sir Arthur Smith.

Earlier in 1953 the choir had its first and only festival at the Royal Festival Hall, which had been built two years before in connection with the Festival of Britain exhibition held on the South Bank of the Thames. Such was the demand for tickets for the evening performance that an afternoon concert was arranged as well. The choir have not used the Festival Hall since because they are not able to book up sufficiently in advance for the extensive arrangements they need to make.

During the same year it was suggested that to consolidate the growing support and prayer for the choir's ministry a Prayer Fellowship should be formed. Since that time it has grown in size and effectiveness, and has enrolled over 500 people. Each one prays for a specific choir member by name, covenanting to pray each day for the ministry of the choir and setting aside the time between 9.00 and 9.30 p.m. on the second Sunday of every third month to join in spirit with other members of the fellowship to pray for the choir. Each member of the fellowship receives each quarter a prayer letter giving details of the choir's forthcoming engagements and news of blessing received during the preceding months. There is no doubt that this very substantial, regular committed prayer support has been a major factor in the choir's continuing ministry.

By this time the choir had built up a regular flow of weekly engagements and was accepting bookings for one or two years in advance, a situation that still prevails. The engagement list supplied to each member at the start of 1953 showed five engagements for April, three for May, four for June, one each for July and September, eight for October, one for November as well as the Carol Festival in December. Nowadays the choir tend to ration themselves to one performance a week generally on Saturday, and no more than one weekend away a month, but occasionally they are able to fit in additional engagements earlier in the week.

The rehearsals had by this time moved to Orange Street Congregational Church behind the National Gallery. The practices still involved a great deal of hard work for Edwin and Muriel Shepherd but by this time the nucleus of the choir had grasped the basic rudiments of singing and some of the excessively hard graft of earlier years was now unnecessary. The familiar cry of 'tenors round the piano', which preceded a session during which the tenors had their parts banged out on the piano in no uncertain terms whilst the rest of the choir enjoyed a breather, was becoming less frequent.

Rehearsals were not without their unrehearsed incidents. About halfway through one practice at Orange Street choir members suddenly became conscious of the smell of smoke which gradually got stronger and stronger until they realised that something very close must be burning. Envoys were despatched from the choir to find out what was happening and they returned with the news that the night-club premises next door to the church, which were separated from them by a narrow passage way, were on fire but that there was no danger to the church premises.

'We'll carry on then,' said Edwin. 'Perhaps the firemen outside will appreciate a bit of Christian music.' But before long they had to abandon their efforts because the smoke and fumes were too great. After pronouncing the benediction Edwin was heard to observe, 'Oh well, the Salvation Army aren't the only ones to go through fire and water – we've only been beaten by the smoke!'

All this time the choir had enjoyed the backing and support of the Christian Endeavour movement not only throughout London but elsewhere. It is doubtful whether it would have been able to establish itself and maintain its support without its faithful backing, but it became obvious during the course of 1953 that the choir was being called to a wider ministry beyond the Christian Endeavour movement and its members were being increasingly drawn from outside the ranks of Endeavourers. In these circumstances it was felt right that there should be a change of name and also a loosening of the ties which bound the choir to the London Christian Endeavour Federation.

There was general agreement that the word chosen to replace 'Endeavour' in the choir's title should if possible start with the same letter so as to preserve continuity.

The subject promoted considerable discussion amongst choir members and others but no readily acceptable alternative was forthcoming until just before Christmas when Edwin and Muriel were sitting by the fire one Sunday afternoon. Muriel looked up from the Bible she was reading and said to her husband, 'I've got a name!'

'So have I, what's yours?'

'I thought "Emmanuel".'

'That's my name too – and it's just right; "God with us". We'll call it the London Emmanuel Choir.' And the London Emmanuel Choir it has been ever since. An attractive typographic design featuring the initials 'LEC' and some notes of music were produced for use on programmes and other choir literature. Although it has subsequently become well-known probably few people outside the choir realise that the notes of music on the design are those to which the word 'Emmanuel' is sung in the carol 'O come, O come, Emmanuel'.

The first opportunity for the new name to be used was at a concert featuring Anton Marco, at one time a member of the Carl Rosa Opera Company, New York, and formerly an atheist. He had been converted and was on a visit to Europe in connection with a European missionary movement. He sang seven solos during the programme, including Albert Hay Malotte's version of the Lord's Prayer – probably one of the first occasions on which it was heard in this country.

There was no Spring Festival in 1954 to avoid clashing with the Billy Graham Greater London Crusade which started at Harringay on March 1st. Edwin had been involved in the musical side of this, the first of the Billy Graham crusades in this country, from the time that Cliff Barrows came over from the United States some months in advance to sound out church leaders and lay the foundations for the running of the crusade. It was natural that Edwin should be asked to serve on the music committee for the crusade and he was actively involved in the preparation of the special songbook produced for that occasion. Members of the choir were urged to join the massed crusade under Cliff Barrows' direction for the duration of the three months of meetings, and all other choir engagements were kept to a minimum, though they did spend the Easter weekend at Bristol during which they sang in the newly-opened Colston Hall. Despite criticism from some church leaders the Graham crusade of 1954 made a tremendous impact on the churches of London, and the Emmanuel Choir was among those who benefited by the increased awareness and enthusiasm of

Christian people and the tremendous part which music played in those meetings.

In the August of the same year the choir had its third holiday, this time at Llandudno, North Wales. They stayed for the fortnight at the Seaforth Hotel, Edwin having been led to this particular establishment through what he regarded as a typical example of the way God's hand was upon him and the choir.

When he was planning the Llandudno holiday he was only able to fit in a short visit to the Welsh resort due to his business commitments. So it was that on a Saturday afternoon in December, 1953, he set out from Euston by train to Llandudno, arriving late in the evening. As he walked from the station into the darkness of a winter's night a high wind howled round his ears and torrential rain lashed the streets. In due course he found the address of the hotel he had been given, at which he was to stay the night, looming large before him dark and forbidding. No light shone from its windows nor was there any sign of life at all. Every door was locked and he was not surprised to learn from the people next door that the hotel was closed. They gave him the address of the town's Baptist minister and at 10 o'clock that night he battled with the wind and rain along a road which seemed to stretch endlessly into the darkness, seeking the man whose address he had been given. When he arrived he sat down to a welcome and surprising hot supper, and a place where he could sleep was found. He was glad to stumble into bed thoroughly exhausted.

He awoke early the following morning and in the course of his Bible reading God gave him the promise, 'Behold, the Lord Thy God hath set the land before thee; go up and possess it, as the Lord God of thy fathers hath said unto thee; fear not neither be discouraged'. (Deuteronomy 1, 21). Downstairs he found a local guide and marked all the hotels large enough for his purpose. After breakfast he made his way to the first one, the Seaforth Hotel, and knocked on the door. The lady who answered the door was dressed to go to church and said that she could not spare the time then but would be happy for him to have lunch with her when they could talk things over. During the lunch he explained what he had in mind. The proprietress, a Christian lady, was very happy with the arrangements and so the matter was settled without further ado.

Edwin felt he had been led very definitely to the Seaforth Hotel and his confidence in the arrangements was fully justified when the choir arrived and spent a very happy holiday at the hotel.

They sang each evening at St. John's Methodist Church. While they were getting ready for the first service a policeman who was watching all the activity taking place outside the church enquired of one of the tenors what was happening. When he heard what it was to be he said scornfully: 'Oh, you'll never fill that place; it hasn't been filled yet.'

'You just come along one night and see,' said the choir member. The constable took up the offer – and had to eat his words. The church was full each night, and such was the demand for the choir that local officials offered the use of the town's bandstand for an open air Saturday night song service when it was calculated that over 1500 people were present.

Whilst they were at Llandudno Muriel Shepherd had a birthday. A splendid cake had already been made beforehand and was transported to Wales with great secrecy, to be revealed at afternoon tea on her birthday. Several choir ladies dressed up in Welsh national costume and the men managed to sing the Welsh national anthem in Welsh for the occasion.

The well-known radio personality Hugh Redwood was the guest speaker at the Spring Festival the following year when he delivered two of his very popular '*Lift up your Hearts*' scripts during the programme of Easter music. Around this time the choir started prison visitation, going to Wandsworth, Wormwood Scrubs and Brixton prisons amongst others. On a visit to the latter the conditions were so cramped that one Sunday the soloist, Victor White, could not climb the steps to the pulpit because the choir was in the way, so he had to clamber in over the back, much to the delight of some of the cat burglars in the audience.

The choir's engagements were taking them farther and farther afield, each visit involving a great deal of hard work behind the scenes quite apart from the musical preparations.

When a letter comes from a church or sponsoring body requesting that the choir should visit a particular place, a reply is sent giving a choice of dates generally one or two years in advance and asking what size choir is required. Experience has shown that at least 60 members are needed at any one engagement for the full benefit of the choir's performance to be felt. When the date has been agreed the engagement is noted in the advanced planning diary. Here the matter rests until some four to five months before the due date. A list of all the forthcoming engagements to which the choir is committed is circulated to all choir members by the secretary in April or May, for engagements from September through to the following June or July, on which they are asked to indicate the dates they can manage. When all the forms are back she compiles a list of the choir members available for each engagement to which she refers when the choir party for a particular visit is being arranged.

The choir is made up in the approximate proportions of one third sopranos, one third contraltos, one sixth tenors and one sixth basses, and those in excess of the numbers required in any one section are told that they will not be required on this occasion. At one time they used to be quite upset if they were not required after having put their name down, but in recent years they have come to accept it without question.

If it is a weekend engagement hospitality has to be arranged for the choir. The names and marital status of all those who are going are forwarded to the person organising the event and he then makes the appropriate arrangement with church members and other interested friends who are prepared to offer hospitality as required. Some organizers see that a letter is subsequently delivered to each choir member notifying them of their host for the weekend, but quite often no one knows where they are going to be staying until they arrive at the engagement. At the end of the Saturday evening meeting there is what is jokingly called in the choir the 'cattle market', when the hosts and hostesses stand on one side of the hall, the choir members on the other and the names are read out in pairs. The introductions are made and hosts and guests go off together for the rest of the evening, sometimes staying up to the early hours of the morning sharing experiences grave and gay.

On one occasion a minister in the area where the choir was singing warned his congregation not to support their meetings. However one particular family from his church not only attended the choir meeting but also gave weekend hospitality to two of the tenors. It was only revealed during the course of discussion late on Saturday evening that the head of the household was Sunday school superintendent of the church where the minister objected to the choir's visit. He was very concerned about spiritual things and as soon as the evening meal was over he opened his heart to the two choir members.

'Why is it I haven't got the same assurance and joy that you folk have?' he asked. 'You folk have got the real thing.'

Tired as the two tenors were they talked about their faith with him until three o'clock in the morning, when he suddenly realised what the time was and bade them goodnight with the parting request that one of them would give a short message to the children at his Sunday school next morning. The opportunity was glady accepted, but just as the school was closing the objecting minister arrived and asked the superintendent what right he had to allow the choir member to preach in his church without permission. The poor superintendent took a good dressing down and was warned never to let it occur again.

On a more light-hearted note a visit to the little village of Stoke Row, near Reading, just off the Kenley to Oxford Road, provided the choir with an experience which has almost become a legend in its time. An annual convention was held there and as there was no hall large enough a marquee was erected on a piece of common land on the outskirts of the village. The organiser, Ray Townsend, managed to produce a larger tent each year the choir went there and on the last occasion he welcomed them with the news that he had got the biggest marquee he could find, but added that it 'leaked like a sieve'.

During the meeting something approaching a cloudburst

descended upon the village and the marquee soon began to let water in at an alarming rate. Those who had had the foresight to bring them hastily produced umbrellas and raincoats. The funniest sight was that of the main speaker, the Rev. George Dempster, diminutive author of *Finding Men for Christ,* sharing an umbrella with the chairman, the Rev. Chalmers Lyon, who was as tall as Dempster was short. The incidental humour of that sight helped to alleviate the distress of those who were not fortunate enough to obtain adequate protection from the rain. The ancient piano was all but ruined and the choir's *Alexander No. 3* hymn books, with their distinctive red covers, got so wet they looked to be dripping blood at one stage in the proceedings; several of them still bear the marks of the deluge to this day.

Fortunately the sun came out before too long and everyone was able to dry out for the evening meeting. This in turn was enlivened by an event which, if the choir's folk lore is to be believed, subsequently happened with alarming frequency, namely, the sudden disappearance of the back row of the male singers whose bench toppled off the edge of the platform. No serious injuries resulted and Edwin Shepherd was heard to remark that the experience should enable the basses to sing some lower notes in future.

By the time the 1955 carol service took place it was necessary to have three performances to cope with the demand for tickets and the Spring Festival the following year had evening performances on Friday and Saturday instead of afternoon and evening ones on Saturday. Susan Harmer and John Clarke presented extracts from *A Pilgrim's Progress* at this festival. Susan was back later in the year with her husband-to-be, Dave Foster, at the carol festival. A talented chalk artist, Dave Foster skilfully built up a picture of the Christmas story with the aid of fluorescent chalks and special lighting. It was widely appreciated by the audience but was viewed by a few of the choir members with some alarm as several of the men had to have their suits cleaned after the festival due to the chalk dust that filled the air following the artist's energetic flourishes.

By this time the choir had become a regular fixture at the Filey Christian Holiday Crusade, having attended the first crusade held in 1955, and it was at Filey that Edwin and Muriel Shepherd heard the Eureka Jubilee Singers, coloured singers from America, who sang at the crusade in 1958. Edwin booked them for the carol festival that year, the first time guest artistes had been invited from outside the circle of singers generally resident in or around London. 'Carols by Candlelight' made its first appearance in the festival programme the same year, led by the Salvation Army Wood Green Citadel Band.

The Spring Festival of 1959 coincided with Edwin and Muriel's silver wedding anniversary. On the Wednesday of festival week they entertained members of the choir and personal friends, numbering some 200, to dinner in the Elizabeth Hall, Soho Square, when they received a presentation on behalf of the choir in the form of a canteen of cutlery. An attractive full colour picture of them taken at Filey appeared on the cover of the programme for the spring festival, which was notable for the inclusion of a personal testimony from Sylvia Smith, a converted teddy-girl.

The choir's piano accordion team made its first public bow at the 1959 Carol Festival. There had always been those among the choir members able to play the accordion and a group was set up to provide the accompaniment for the Carols by Candlelight feature at the Christmas festival and community chorus-singing on visits elsewhere. The festival also introduced the *Zither Carol*, Sir Malcolm Sargent's arrangement of the Czech folk tune with attractive words and a catchy rhythm.

The choir had by this time established a reputation for leading the way so far as evangelical music was concerned and as they broadened their repertoire and became more versatile their music increasingly suited all tastes, a fact which was illustrated by the demand for pieces they had sung which followed their visit to a particular locality. Church choirs which had been singing the same old anthems, oratorios and Gospel songs for years were being introduced to a whole new range of music which was well within their ability, but of which they had been unaware.

As if to show that the tried and tested oratorio Olivet to Calvary was not beneath them, however, the choir performed J. H. Maunder's well-known work in its entirety at their Spring Festival in 1960. This was a particularly nostalgic occasion for Edwin and Muriel Shepherd as it recalled to them their first choral venture over 20 years before at the little Baptist Church in Silvertown.

After five successive years at the Filey Christian Holiday Crusade Edwin decided the choir should break new ground for their holiday venture in 1960 and so it was that on an evening in late May (holidays are taken early for the convenience of the large number of teachers in the choir who utilise their half-term holidays) a party of choir members boarded the boat at Liverpool after a long train journey from London and crossed the Irish Sea to Dun Laoghaire. They approached the Republic of Ireland with some misgivings as they were conscious that the Roman Catholic faith was predominant there and Protestantism was very thin on the ground, but their doubts vanished when the first evening engagement was packed to capacity and additional seats had to be arranged. This happened again and again, and by the time they rode into Dublin by coach to be received by the Lord Mayor himself they felt sure that God was blessing their ministry.

The Lord Mayor, a practising Roman Catholic, was charming and generous to a fault and left them in no doubt as to the warmth of the welcome he extended, even though they felt obliged to spurn part of his proferred hospitality – two large trays of alcoholic drinks!

On the first Sunday evening of their stay they sang in the YMCA building in Dublin, which held 1100 people. It was completely full for the occasion and when the time came for the concert to end cries of 'More, more!' were heard from the audience, much to the surprise of the organisers who had advised a prompt finish in view of the attractions to the young people present offered by moon-lit walks along the riverside. So the holiday continued with packed audiences wherever they went. At Arklow, a little seaside resort south of Greystones where they were staying, the vast audience rose to its feet and stood in silent appreciation as the choir filed out of the hall at the end of the meeting.

Chapter 5

A GROWING VISION

Two missionaries in the heart of inland Africa were returning from a far distant village to their base. The sticky heat and their weariness kept them silent and as they plodded on in the gathering darkness only the sounds of animal and insect night-life could be heard. Suddenly they both stood still. Coming through the trees, faint but distinct, was the sound of a great choir singing. They looked at one another in amazement, dumbfounded. They were almost ready to believe that the angelic host which sang to the shepherds at Bethlehem had paid them a return visit. They hurried on and as they approached the mission station the music grew louder. Someone at the station was playing a tape recording of the London Emmanuel Choir just received from a friend at home.

During the months which followed that tape was played over and over again as a reminder of the unity of all true believers in Christ and the reality of the prayers and practical interest which choir members and other friends had in the work of the lone missionaries in their remote station.

For several years the choir's carol festivals had been tape recorded by Frank Birkenshaw, who in the late 1950s had left the publishing firm of Marshall, Morgan and Scott to set up his own publishing and recording organisation in part of a disused church in Camberwell. The tapes had been copied and sent out to missionaries overseas with whom the choir had been in touch in the past.

It is difficult for those living in the comfort of British home life with radio, television and record player ready to hand to realise the isolation felt by such missionaries, particularly those cut off from contact with anything remotely resembling Western civilisation. One young missionary who spent several years in the Brazilian interior, was typical of those in such circumstances who valued the arrival of a London Emmanuel Choir tape.

'If only people could know what those tapes did for me,' she wrote on one occasion. 'I was utterly cut off from any contact, except by letter from my own people and I was living day after day with those who could not speak my language. Sometimes the loneliness became unbearable and at such moments I would put on one of the tapes. It was as if God himself was speaking just to me. My world changed. To play "Remember me O Mighty One" was to know I was not any longer alone. He was with me and every member of the London Emmanuel Choir was with me.

'What cared I that all manner of noxious insects were crawling around the little jungle house, that the jungle itself was creeping inch by inch towards me, that the damp miasma was the enemy of my typewriter, corroding it with mildew and dust. I too sang "When lone my watch I'm keeping, remember me O Mighty One". Spiritual strength and physical strength were given back to me and I rejoiced again – and got on with the job.'

By this time the choir could look back on 15 years of increasing usefulness in the service of God. The raw collection of untrained amateur singers with which the choir had started had been groomed into a well disciplined, technically competent and musically inspiring choir which could hold its own with the best in the land, but its ministry was limited by the physical limitations of the strength, energy and time of the choir and its leaders. With engagements all over London and the Home Counties virtually every weekend and with monthy trips farther afield the choir was reaching thousands of people with the Christian message in song, but Edwin Shepherd realised that the choir could not stand still and if its development and growth was to continue there would have to be an extension of its ministry.

The tape recordings of the choir were obviously useful in this respect but in the late 1950s tape recorders were comparatively few and far between. The industrial revolution in Japan which was to flood the market in the mid-sixties with cheap tape recorders and other electronic gadgetry had not then taken place. But many people had record players, or as they were commonly called in those days, gramophones. The great LP boom was just starting to revolutionise the record industry. The old 78s with their high cost and short duration were giving way to the smaller cheaper 45 rpm 'singles' and EPs and the full-size long-playing records which provided up to 45 minutes' music without the bother of constantly changing records.

As far back as 1950 the choir had made three 78 rpm records of hymns issued by Evangelical Recordings, and by the end of 1957 they had added five more, this time produced by Pilgrim Recordings, the newly established recording division of Marshall, Morgan and Scott. It was natural, therefore, that Pilgrim should be entrusted with the choir's first two ten-inch L.P.s released in 1958 and 1960. They were an immediate success and proved to be the forerunners of a continuing stream of first class L.P.s which have not only helped to increase the scope of the choir's ministry, but have themselves been responsible for raising the standard of choral singing in this country amongst evangelical churches.

A stategic year for the choir was 1962 for several reasons. For one thing it was the year in which Edwin Shepherd retired from the bank after 42 years' service. When he left he occupied the highly responsible position of chief clerk in one of London's leading branches. There is little doubt that had he been prepared to devote more time to his banking career and had not filled his spare time with unceasing Christian activity of one sort or another he would have risen higher in the bank than he actually did. But he always made it clear that his ambition was to serve the Lord and that provided his employment was such as to give him the freedom he needed out of office hours to engage in Christian service this was all he wanted. He had never sought advancement for its own sake within the bank. Indeed at one time he was in charge of a branch for several months as a result of the promotion of the then manager, but someone else was appointed as the new manager in due course and he was quite happy to step down.

One of his great hopes upon retiring was that the

additional time he would have available for Christian work would enable him to increase the effectiveness and development of the choir even more. His first move was to take a fresh look at the Christmas festivals. For some time his contacts with the huge American religious recording industry had been strengthening. Music played a much larger part in American church life than it did in Britain and consequently there was no lack of instrumentalists, vocalists and talented musicians of many different styles over there.

One of the names most widely respected in these circles was that of Pat Zondervan, President of Singspiration Incorporated which was responsible for a great deal of evangelical music both in the field of publishing and records. On one occasion he said to Edwin, 'If you should ever think of having an American artiste at one of your festivals, let me know. I've got just the person.' So it was natural that Edwin should first turn to him for help when he decided the time was right for this further expansion of the choir's activities. He suggested Bette Stalnecker, who had made a considerable name for herself as a solo artist on record, radio and television, so it was agreed that she should be the guest artiste for the festival in 1962.

In order to cope with the anticipated increase in demand for tickets, and because the four performances held in previous years were still insufficient to meet the needs of the thousands who wanted to attend the carol festival, the number of performances was increased to five that year.

The colossal task of dispatching ticket application forms and allocating tickets for the festivals is handled by members of the choir themselves, working almost round the clock during the peak periods. The mailing list comprises approximately seven thousand names and addresses to whom are sent twice each year application forms for tickets for the spring and carol festivals. When the application forms have been printed the task of inserting them into ready addressed envelopes begins. Choir members volunteer to assist in this task and the envelopes are sealed and stamped for posting. An individual stamp is stuck on each letter because this is the only way the post office is prepared to accept them for posting all on the same day. If the letters were franked or handled as bulk mail there would be no guarantee that the letters would go out at one and the same time and this would mean that some people would receive their ticket application forms possibly after all the tickets had been sold, so fast is the reaction of early ticket purchasers.

The application forms are normally sent out on a Wednesday in September for the Carol Festival and in February for the Spring Festival. On the following Monday as many as 800 forms may be returned in one post to 34 Buckles Way and the mail is opened by a team of volunteers, the money is separated and noted on the application form and the forms are then placed in separate boxes for each performance in order of receipt day by day during the week they come in. At the end of the week the first allocation of seats is made. A room is hired in Central London in which a team starts on Monday morning at nine o'clock and works a full-day each day until the job is done, going through all the application forms in order of their receipt, allocating the tickets and marking them off on the huge seating plans.

It sounds easy enough but the difficulty is that the Saturday evening performance is probably sold out before the requirements of the first day's applications have all been met, so that people have to be given their second choice, or as the process goes on sometimes their third or fourth choice. Perhaps the price of ticket they require has sold out and they therefore have to have cheaper ones and a refund has to be made. After the first few days all five performances are more or less sold out and the rest of the time is spent sending back money and making refunds.

Over the years people have gradually realised that either they have to book by return to get any chance at all of Saturday evening seats or else they must opt straightaway for seats at other performances. Much thought has been given to the possibility of making more seats available, particularly at the Carol Festival, to ease the disappointment felt by as many as 6000 people who are sometimes unable to get seats, but the difficulty is that no other hall is available in Central London for the number of nights required and to increase the number of performances at the Central Hall would be virtually a physical impossibility. All that can be done is to make sure the forms are dealt with strictly in rotation so that preference is given to people who reply immediately.

Choir members are given very few privileges so far as tickets are concerned. They are permitted to have only two tickets each for the Saturday evening performance and they order all other tickets on the same date and terms as members of the public, when they receive their application forms in the general mailing.

As expected, the 1962 Carol Festival was a complete sell-out, the promised appearance of Bette Stalnecker being eagerly anticipated by the choir supporters. She was due to arrive on the Tuesday before the festival started and a reception had been laid on to welcome her to London. However fog hung over London all day and Heathrow Airport was closed. Her plane was diverted and she could not get to London in time for the reception but it was hoped she would arrive the following day. The fog persisted throughout Wednesday and when the time came for the first performance that evening there was still no sign of her.

The programme went ahead as planned and when the time came for her first solo Edwin Shepherd explained the difficulties she had encountered on her journey and called upon Dick Anthony, her accompanist who was fortunately already in London, to provide a musical interlude. The programme continued and there was still no sign of her. It was almost time for her second solo when suddenly she swept into view through the side door and on to the platform still wearing her travelling outfit and outwardly calm despite the delays and discomforts she had suffered on her journey.

She sang her full repertoire and finished with an interpretation of the Russian hymn, 'How Great Thou Art' which was talked about for a long time afterwards. She had learnt the language used by deaf and dumb people and as she sang the stirring words of the hymn so her hands 'spoke' the words for the benefit of those who could not hear.

So great had been the demand for the first choir record a

year before that another was produced especially for this festival comprising excerpts from the previous year's festival together with pieces recorded at other times by the choir under the general title *Come Carolling*.

At the beginning of 1963 Edwin Shepherd took stock of the situation in which he found himself. The effectiveness of the choir's ministry showed no signs of diminishing. After every visit they made, stories of conversion, re-dedication, encouragement and blessing as a result of the choir flooded in through the letterbox at 34 Buckles Way. Indeed opening and reading the breakfast mail each morning – something he could now do without having to rush out to catch the train to work – was one of the aspects of leading the choir he found most rewarding.

'I have only known the London Emmanuel Choir in comparatively recent years,' wrote one middle-aged man, 'but I can assure you that it was, under God, one of the main things that kept me on course in the darkness a few years ago. It was a light from heaven in a very great personal darkness'.

An eight-year-old boy wrote to say that 'due to the singing done by your choir I found a Friend who will stay with me. I thought I would just like to let you know.' In his answering letter Edwin Shepherd told him how wonderful it was that he had 'found the Lord Jesus as your Saviour last Saturday evening. This is a wonderful thing, and I am sure that you will never regret having committed your life to Him. Be sure to read your Bible every day, just a little portion, and always remember to say your prayers and ask God to guide you throughout your life, and I am sure you will experience much blessing always.' The boy no doubt treasures that letter just as much as his is valued and preserved in the choir's correspondence files.

Another letter writer described the effect of the choir's singing to him: 'Your concerts are oases – places of rest and recuperation. To sit and listen to your choir is food for my soul.' While yet another told how a particular record had been sent by a mother, who was separated from her husband, a member of the Exclusive Brethren, to her disillusioned son in New Zealand who had thoroughly backslidden. When he heard the record something in the music went straight to his heart and he came back to God.

So it went on. Letter after letter told of God's blessing through the choir's ministry. (Not all letters were couched in the same high spiritual tone. One he received from a lady shortly after he had casually mentioned at a meeting that they would like to sing with an orchestra, is reported to have said: 'Please can I join your orchestra? I have always wanted to fiddle for God'!) How much greater blessing there would be, he felt, if church choirs and other local singing groups could catch the vision of musical evangelism as practised by the Emmanuel Choir. In travelling round the country with the choir his worst fears about the low level of evangelical music in churches had been confirmed. He was sure that this in part helped to explain the tremendous response which the choir elicited from audiences. They had not heard anything like it for years and this, Edwin felt, was largely due to the lack of imagination and resources at the disposal of the average church choir.

So he set to work to bring to fruition his great dream, to inspire other evangelical choirs to attempt the type of music which the Emmanuel Choir had sung so successfully and to encourage them to widen their range and increase their effectiveness through the singing of simple, tuneful melodies to scriptural words.

In his contacts with other people concerned with the development of evangelical music it became clear that the way forward was to organise a huge festival of evangelical choirs in London, the proceeds from which would help to finance the purchase of the music used in the festival and present it free of charge to the participating choirs for their subsequent use. The Royal Albert Hall was booked for June 13th, 1964, and letters of invitation were sent out to choirs attached to evangelical churches throughout southern England. The response was immediate and overwhelming. Some 32 choirs including the London Emmanuel Choir indicated they would like to take part from Lowestoft and Norwich in the east to Weston-Super-Mare and Wiveliscombe in the west, and around 20 choirs who applied later than the others had to be turned down because a thousand voice choir was already assured by the initial response, and even Edwin Shepherd did not think he could cope with anything much bigger.

Meanwhile preparations for the 1963 carol festival occupied the choir on their return from their second holiday in the Emerald Isle, this time to Northern Ireland to sing at the annual convention of the Irish Alliance of Christian Workers Union. There were seldom less than a thousand people to hear them sing each evening and on one occasion in the open-air the audience exceeded 1500. After the convention there were engagements at Ballymena, Londonderry and Lisburn. On their return one choir member commented, 'It was such a humbling experience to find churches packed to capacity and hundreds of people unable to gain entrance. It made us ask "Why has the Lord sought *us* out in this way?" Then we got upon our knees in thanksgiving that we were His instruments and determined to do more, much more.'

The guest artiste at the Carol Festival was John Stuart Anderson, a young British actor, who presented *The Spirit of Christmas*, part of a series of presentations under the general title *The Living Word*. During the previous six years over 700 performances of *The Living Word* had been given in cathedrals, concert halls, theatres and churches of many different denominations. He had gone on an American tour in 1961 and everywhere he went audiences had been enraptured by his command of the spoken word and the dramatic intensity with which he put across the message.

At the Spring Festival the choir extended a welcome to their second artiste from America, Glenn Jorian, one of whose distinctions had been to record a song singing all four parts. He was to return to the Central Hall on two subsequent occasions, in 1966 with fellow singer Claire Hess and a year later with Ray Felton and Bill Pearce as the Melody Four.

Immediately after the Spring Festival the practice for the Albert Hall festival started in earnest so that each choir was competent to sing the pieces and was aware of the requirements of Edwin Shepherd as conductor before the choirs were brought together. So during the early months of 1964 Edwin and Muriel sped round southern England meeting the participating choirs at a dozen or so area practices and putting them through their paces.

It was exhausting work, and something which could never have been undertaken during Edwin's active business life, but he found it tremendously rewarding as the choirs responded to the opportunity to sing for the first time music which was within their range but outside the general run of pieces to which they had become accustomed. Not only were they thus introduced to new music but they also captured something of the enthusiasm and dedication of Edwin Shepherd himself as he sought to interpret the music to them.

Chapter 6

LET THE WHOLE WORLD SING

Saturday June 13th, 1964 dawned bright and clear and all was set for the great festival of praise in the Royal Albert Hall. Many of the participating choirs set out at crack of dawn from the far west to arrive in London in time for the afternoon rehearsal, the only time when the choirs would sing together before the evening performance. All went well and as the time for the start of the festival drew near hundreds upon hundreds of people from London and the Home Counties converged upon the auditorium. As the audience took their seats they read the programme notes which Edwin Shepherd had penned to explain the purpose behind the festival.

'It is devised to bring together those Christian choirs which are interested in the work of evangelising through the ministry of music and by mutual edification to raise the standard of Gospel singing,' he wrote. 'The musical appreciation of our generation is so high that a crude presentation of the glorious message of salvation serves to repel rather than attract those to whom it is addressed. Nothing but the best will do, yet for too long our churches have been satisfied with indifferent choral singing and this wider field of attractive evangelism has been neglected.

'If this festival stirs up new enthusiasm amongst the singers, and succeeds in discovering new arrangements of well loved hymns and anthems for use throughout the country, a great purpose will have been served: but better still if, thereby, gifted men and women hear the call to serve the Lord in a ministry that can be blessed to all, the Kingdom of God will be extended and the testimony of Jesus Christ gloriously proclaimed to a dying world.'

To assist the congregational singing the music of all four hymns to be sung by the audience was included in the programme, including the twentieth-century hymn-tune for 'At the Name of Jesus every knee shall bow'. The sheer thrill of singing aloud the praises of God in such a vast company remained with many people long after the festival ended. For those singing in the massed choir the experience must have been even greater as they responded to the leading of their conductor.

As the echo of the final hymn 'Forward be our watchword' died away Edwin Shepherd realised that he had entered yet another, altogether more significant phase of his life's work. God had raised him up for such a time as this to recall the churches of the land to a fresh appreciation of the part that music could play in the worship of God and the evangelising of those without Christ.

As he had hoped, the income from the tickets for the festival provided sufficient funds for all the music used for it to be given free of charge to the singers who had taken part, with the result that the repertoires of some 30 choirs were greatly enlarged at no extra cost to themselves. Furthermore as a direct result of the festival church choirs in several areas within reasonable distance of each other got together and reproduced similar local festivals, thus encouraging within their own locality the idea of using a more popular form of Gospel music acceptable to those outside the church as well as to those within. There was evidence of a renewed enthusiasm for evangelical music and in many other ways the festival served to stimulate an interest in such music far in excess of anything which the Emmanuel Choir had been able to achieve on its own.

A tentative date for a second festival had been announced even before the first one was held, and the response was so great that preparations were immediately put in hand to make the second festival bigger and better than the first.

All this additional work and effort did not detract Edwin Shepherd from his commitment to the on-going work of the Emmanuel Choir, however, and at the Carol Festival in 1964 he attempted what was the choir's single most ambitious project up to that time, a rendering of the Christmas Cantata *Night of Miracles* by the American composer John Peterson. This marked a further step forward in the increasingly close co-operation between the choir and Pilgrim Recordings, the record division of Marshall, Morgan and Scott, who released a British edition of the American recording of the cantata orchestrated and conducted by Ralph Carmichael.

This year was also the first occasion when Mrs. Mary Wilson, wife of the then Prime Minister was present. The invitation to attend the festival came through the *Sunday Companion* who published an article about her shortly after Harold Wilson became Prime Minister. Mary Wilson herself was the daughter of a Congregational minister and both she and her husband were in membership at Hampstead Garden Suburb Free Church in North London. She took a great interest in the choir from then on and was a regular attender at the carol festivals, going backstage after the performances to have coffee with the Shepherds. She used to get on particularly well with Edwin, often chatting to him for quite a while.

Due to continuing demand for tickets for the Spring Festival the following year the number of performances was extended to three, Thursday, Friday and Saturday. Meanwhile anticipation was building up for the second Festival of Evangelical Mixed Voice Choirs to be held on Saturday, June 19th. Just as before Edwin and Muriel set out on numerous journeys to meet the choirs taking part in the festival, guiding them through the music which he had carefully chosen for the programme and encouraging them to make the second festival even better than the first. And so it turned out to be. With harp solos from Frances Mon Jones, wife of a Welsh Methodist minister, dramatic presentations from Nigel Goodwin, a young Christian actor, and a stirring epilogue from Lindsay Glegg, a continual supporter of any and every activity of the Emmanuel Choir, the festival once more touched the hearts of all present and sent them on their way determined to 'Let the song go round the earth, Jesus Christ is Lord.'

Bette Stalnecker paid a return visit to the festival that year and fortunately her travelling arrangements went without a hitch. She bought with her not only her husband Ed, but also authority from her home city, Memphis, Tennessee, to confer the freedom of the city upon Edwin Shepherd and a certificate and keys making him an honorary citizen of Lake Charles, Louisiana. 1965 also saw the introduction of Father Christmas into the programme for the first time. Edwin always used to say, 'We can't repeat the same thing each year, however successful. The people like something fresh.' So he persuaded the two men in the piano accordion team, John Cook and his son Mervyn, to dress up as Father Christmas to introduce the 'Carols by Candlelight'.

Edwin always timed the programme meticulously and there was little time for ad-libbing, so for the first three performances John Cook confined himself to the immediate task of introducing the carols with virtually no comment on the side, although he liked to 'get across' to the audience when possible as he felt it created a better response. On the Saturday morning he lay in bed contemplating the afternoon and evening programmes, turning over in his mind one or two humorous ideas and wondering if he dare steal the time to introduce them. He decided he had better not. As they were about to go on to the platform for the community singing one of the girls in the team said, 'There are ever so many children out there, John. You'd better say something to them.' Then after a pause she added 'You'd better explain why there are two of you as Father Christmas'.

John had not thought of that. No one had foreseen that it might give rise to awkward questions. Rather nervously he decided to take the plunge and when he got out on to the platform he launched into an explanation that years ago in fairyland a baby Father Christmas had been born who grew up like ordinary boys and girls and was learning to take over from him when he really was too old. He said he was his son (which was true) and he'd brought him along to meet the boys and girls and here he was. He then went on to talk about their letters and promised to deliver their presents but explained he might be a little late as he was having trouble with his reindeer. The culprit, he said, was Rudolph the Red-nosed Reindeer and the team were demanding more hay and shorter flowers!

Edwin joined in the laughter with everyone else, calling

out 'Well done, brother' at one stage. During tea time he left his table and went across to John Cook and said 'I want you to repeat what you said this afternoon. Do more and no less'. John started to apologise for breaking the 'rules' but he waived the explanation aside with the comment, 'This is a happy occasion. We mustn't be all seriousness. It's good to have a laugh now and again.' So Father Christmas came to stay, and has been virtually a fixture since.

Before the Stalneckers returned to the USA they visited Edwin and Muriel's home in Banstead. Ed Stalnecker had been very impressed by the choir at his first visit. 'When I decided to visit your shores I expected to find a large choir, and I expected to find a good choir.' he said, 'but since I knew that it was composed of volunteer people throughout I did not expect to find an absolutely professional quality group, such as you have got here. This has surprised me tremendously, because I have not heard a choir singing the Gospel set to music anywhere in the United States to touch the London Emmanuel Choir.'

With praise like that ringing in their ears and their American contacts strengthening each year, it was hardly surprising that suggestions started to be made with increasing frequency that the choir should visit America. Edwin Shepherd took a lot of persuading. On several previous occasions he had tried to make arrangements for the choir to go overseas and on each occasion nothing had come of it. Did this, he wondered, suggest that the choir's ministry was to be in the United Kingdom only? He and his wife prayed about it a great deal. Muriel was very keen that the choir should go and when yet more invitations came to them, Edwin at last decided it was the right thing for them to do.

Scores of letters were typed to various contacts they had in the States and when some of them produced no response fresh letters were sent in an effort to make the best use of their stay and draw up as full an itinerary as possible.

The Billy Graham Earls' Court Crusade also took place during 1966. It was an indication of the growth in stature of both the choir and its leader since Billy Graham last conducted a major London crusade in 1955 that Edwin was appointed chairman of the music committee responsible both for drawing up the hymnbook and organising the crusade choir. In a letter of thanks to Edwin after the crusade finished, Cliff Barrows, the Billy Graham team songleader, wrote:

'Words could not begin to express the gratitude of my heart and the privilege that was mine of working with you in the ministry of music for the London crusade. The experience of those weeks will always live in my memory as I look back and remember what God has wrought through the ministry of song and the preaching of His word.

'Your leadership as chairman of the music committee meant more to any of us on the team and to me personally than I could ever tell you. I do want to thank you from the bottom of my heart for your untiring labour of love, your cheerfulness of spirit and the encouragement of your presence night after night.'

That year the choir celebrated its 21st birthday, and for the last three days in July the choir members invaded the residential conference centre of High Leigh, Hoddesdon, for a retreat. Only twelve of those present had been in the original choir in 1945 and they kept the other choir members entertained with lively stories about those early days in the choir. This was followed later in the autumn by an anniversary dinner for 250 guests at the Criterion restaurant near Piccadilly Circus with Lindsay Glegg as guest of honour and Maj.-Gen. Wilson Haffenden giving one of the speeches. The *Sunday Companion* presented them with a beautifully iced cake and, said Edwin, in a letter to one of the Billy Graham team afterwards, 'It really was something quite on the Billy Graham style.'

A thanksgiving service for the 21st anniversary was held in the Central Hall on November 15th that year. Three of those who had been closest to the choir throughout its history took part, Lindsay Glegg, Douglas White and the Rev. Eric Wood. Many people were disappointed to see so many empty seats in the hall. This was because Edwin Shepherd had decided against issuing tickets for the service for fear that it would become just another festival. Unfortunately without the assurance of a seat that a ticket would have given them many people decided not to come up to London for the service assuming there would be no room for them.

But any disappointment the Shepherds may have felt in that context was more than compensated for by the large number of letters and telephone calls they subsequently received, not only telling of the blessing that particular service had been to them, but also thanking God for all 21 years of the choir's ministry. One letter particularly appealed to Edwin's sense of humour. It came from an osteopath in South Croydon, Surrey, who concluded his letter, 'My wife Mary wonders how Mrs. Shepherd managed to keep relaxed sitting all evening without a back rest.'

'It would take an osteopath's wife to notice Mrs. Shepherd sits without a back to her seat the whole of the evening,' wrote Edwin in reply. 'This is part of her dedication to the work of the choir and very few people realise it or notice it, but of course it is quite something.'

During the autumn another batch of letters had to be typed about the American trip. The proposed itinerary was beginning to take shape. It included Buffalo, London, Ontario, Detroit, Grand Rapids, Chicago, Washington, Collingswood and Hawthorn, New Jersey, and New York, but the response was slow coming back. In a letter to Lee Fisher, an American friend, in November 1966 Edwin described 1966 as 'the busiest year I have ever known. It is all very well being 21 years old, but when the celebrations nearly kill you it is hardly worth it!'

During that year the choir became a charitable trust and a board of trustees was formed to take major decisions affecting the running of the choir. Financially the choir had always been self-supporting and Edwin and Muriel Shepherd were proud of the fact that they had never needed to ask the public for money. From its earliest days the income received from the sale of tickets at the festivals was used to finance the provision of music for the choir. As funds grew, added to by royalties from records and proceeds from the sale of records at their own engagements, so the money was ploughed back into providing the choir with more music.

The travelling expenses of choir members who had to make journeys of excessive length to attend practices and other engagements were met by the choir funds and the only other major expense was the payment for guest artistes at the choir's major festivals. These expenses were sometimes heavy if soloists came from America or elsewhere overseas, as they were treated generously during their stay in London. There were virtually no administrative costs apart from telephones, stationery, postage and other small items.

Amidst all this extra work the 1966 Carol Festival came and went. It was notable for the presence of Peter Baillie, an outstanding tenor soloist from New Zealand who was singing for a season in Austria and flew over to London for the festival. In response to popular demand the *Night of Miracles* cantata by John Peterson was repeated.

During the early part of 1967 final arrangements were being made for the American tour. The final plan, somewhat expanded from the original schedule, was to leave Gatwick Airport on Saturday, May 27th and fly to New York, there picking up two coaches and visiting Boston, Cambridge, Montreal, Ottawa, Toronto, Niagara, Ann Arbor, Grand Rapids, Chicago, Richmond, Washington, Philadelphia and Atlantic City, returning to New York City on Friday, June 9th, and flying back to London the following day. The choir was to charter a plane for the flight across the Atlantic as this would be the cheapest way per person, and they were arranging to hire two 39 seater coaches to take them on the 2300 mile round-trip for their performances. Each choir member was to pay £100 to cover his own travelling expenses, but the remaining costs were to be met by their hosts.

There was no shortage of volunteers for the American trip when it was initially proposed but by the time the final arrangements came to be made there were just about the right number, 78, needed to make the trip. A special feature so far as the choir was concerned was to be that words of all pieces sung during the tour would be learnt by heart, a refinement which Edwin thought would be appreciated in the States.

Above: A bicycle made for three – at the Filey Christian Holiday Crusade. Edwin with two of the choir members.

Below: Memories of Harringay. Three of the Billy Graham team (left to right), Tedd Smith, George Beverley Shea and Cliff Barrows, with Edwin at Filey, 1956.

Photo: Pat Thomas, A.R.P.S., A.M.P.A.

Above: Ten years later, Edwin again with Bev. Shea, this time at Earl's Court, London, during the 1966 Billy Graham Crusade.

Below: The scene in the Royal Albert Hall on June 13th, 1964,

Photo: Peter Thomas.

Above: Behind the scenes the team of volunteers prepare to dispatch thousands of ticket application forms for the 1966 carol festival.

the First Festival of Evangelical Mixed Voice Choirs.

Photo: Douglas F. Lawson, F.I.I.P., F.R.P.S., F.R.M.S.

Above: One of his last public performances; Edwin conducts the Fourth Festival of Evangelical Choirs at the Royal Albert Hall, October, 1970.

Below: Celebrating the choir's 25th birthday; Edwin and Muriel ceremonially cut the cake at the anniversary dinner at the Criterion Restaurant, London, a few days later.

Photo: Douglas F. Lawson, F.I.I.P., F.R.P.S., F.R.M.S.

One Sunday in the early part of February Edwin and Muriel were going for a short walk from their home at Banstead when Muriel noticed that Edwin could only walk slowly and needed to hold on to her arm. They had to stop while he sat down for a bit.

'You ought to go and see the doctor, dear,' said Muriel.

'Oh, it's only my bronchitis,' said Edwin.

Muriel said nothing more on that occasion but a few days later they were due to go to their doctor for preliminary injections in connection with the American trip. Edwin had his injection first and then went into the house for a cup of tea with the doctor's wife, Eileen – they were friends of the family. While Muriel was having her injection she said to the doctor, 'Edwin has got a nasty cough.' He studied her face carefully and noted the anxiety in her tone. He scribbled on a piece of paper on his desk.

'Here,' he said, 'Take this form and tell him to be X-rayed.'

Edwin went up to the hospital to be X-rayed and thought nothing more of it until a few days later when the doctor telephoned and asked him to go and see him. He came straight to the point.

'You've got to rest for three months,' he told him. 'You've got an enlarged heart, and unless you ease up a bit there'll be nothing I can do for you.'

Edwin returned home to break the news to Muriel. Together they faced the agonising decision about the American trip Edwin was to have signed the contract for £6000 to charter the aircraft the previous week, but there had been a delay on the American side. He was due to sign it two days after the doctor broke the news. A visiting specialist made it quite clear that he could not go to America so the trip was cancelled, to everyone's intense disappointment.

He had to go into a London hospital for a fortnight's treatment during which he lost so much weight that he hardly looked the same man when he came out. Then followed convalescence at Bournemouth and a period of rest at home. Countless letters had to be written to his American contacts explaining the situation and cancelling the arrangements.

He made such good progress towards a full recovery that the doctor allowed him to conduct the Spring Festival at the end of April. Muriel conducted the choir for all the other engagements until the summer, and a choir member took over as accompanist.

After a further period of holiday he seemed to all intents and purposes to be back to his normal self again, though he was never again to recapture the fullness of face which was such a characteristic of his earlier days. In fact, he allowed very few people to realise it, but he himself knew full well that he was living on borrowed time.

Chapter 7

INDIAN SUMMER OF A SHEPHERD

'I've got Harold to come at last.' Edwin Shepherd easily recognised the voice on the other end of the phone. It was Mary Wilson, highly delighted because she had at last managed to persuade her husband to come with her to the 1967 Carol Festival. She had been each year since her first visit in 1964, either with one of her sons or with a friend, and the news that the Prime Minister was to attend the festival gave a tremendous fillip to the choir in their preparations. Ben and Beth Allen were the guest artistes from America, playing guitar and Irish harp respectively (Ben Allen returned to the Central Hall in 1969 with the Laymen Singers who were the choir's guests at the Spring Festival), and the choir performed another of John Peterson's Christmas cantatas, *Born a King,* subsequently released on record.

The next milestone for the choir was the production of their first record with orchestral accompaniment. The idea of such a record first came up in a conversation Edwin and Muriel had with Raymond Moseley, a professional musician and a director of Westminster Sinfonia Productions Ltd., who provided session musicians for recording work or even a full orchestra or sections of an orchestra as required. He had coffee with the Shepherds at Heathrow Airport one day in 1967 when they were seeing off some American artistes who had been in this country for a recording session with the Westminster Sinfonia Orchestra, of which Raymond Moseley was the leader. He had heard the choir sing quite recently and had been very impressed with their performance, but mentioned how much better he thought they would sound if they had an orchestral backing.

Edwin was very taken with the idea and questioned Raymond Moseley closely about his orchestra and what arrangements would need to be made if the choir was to record with them. He thought about it for a long time after this. Perhaps this was the significant move forward which he felt the choir needed to make in his ceaseless quest for progress and development. When he had made up his mind to go ahead with the idea he telephoned Raymond Moseley and between them they set the ball rolling. Gareth Davies, the very talented musical director of the long-running West End stage success, *Fiddler on the Roof*, was recommended by Raymond Moseley as the best man to do the orchestration and in due course the four of them met to discuss the content of the record. The new orchestrations which were eventually forthcoming meant that the choir had to learn completely new parts for the recording session, but eventually all was ready for the record to be made.

As it turned out they chose one of the coldest days of the winter to make the recording, and St. Michael's Church, Highgate, North London, where the recording was made, did not improve matters. Everybody was wearing their winter coats, and Marie Goosens, one of the famous musical family, wore a fur coat while she was playing the harp. Fortunately the whole thing was over in one day; in the morning they recorded the pieces which had brass backing and in the afternoon with the string section. The record was subsequently issued in June of that year under the title *Whispering Hope* and was an immediate success.

By way of a change the guests at the Spring Festival that year came from Sweden. The four-piece close harmony Gospel group and three musicians brought a touch of sunny Scandinavia to the Central Hall.

After a break of three years the third Festival of Evangelical Choirs was planned for June 15th, 1968. No fewer than 39 choirs took part this time, and once more there were the exhausting treks across the country for Edwin and Muriel to meet the choirs taking part and put them through their paces. Tim and Doreen Buckley and their son David were among the guest artistes at the Albert Hall festival and Pat Zondervan, of the American publishing house, happened to be in the country at the time and took part, reading a passage of scripture. Lindsay Glegg was there once again to lead in prayer and pronounce the benediction.

Hardly had he done the latter when Edwin turned to the audience and in the inspiration of the moment invited them to join with the choirs in singing an unscheduled extra piece, 'God be with you till we meet again'.

The summer of 1969 was a busy one for the choir for in June they recorded their second L.P. with orchestral backing, this time in the Olympic Studios in London. The musical arrangements were again by Gareth Davies and the Westminster Sinfonia Orchestra with Raymond Moseley. *Let the whole world know* was issued in October that year and was another best seller.

Two months after recording it the choir were back in the recording studios once more, this time the CTS studios in London, reputed to be among the finest in the country. It was to be a 'show-case' album for Marion Redwood, who had been a soloist with the choir from shortly after she first joined in 1962, but the choir supplied the backing together with the strings and rhythm of the Westminster Sinfonia under the direction of an old friend and organ accompanist of the choir, George Blackmore, who also did the musical arrangements. This was the first time Marion's voice had been given the sort of choral and orchestral backing it so richly deserved. No other choir soloist had been so widely appreciated in the choir both in terms of the quality of her voice and the meaning which she gave to the words.

The guest soloist for the 1969 Carol Festival was again Peter Baillie the young New Zealand tenor who had served the choir so well three years before. A non-musical feature of that festival was the unveiling of what was claimed to be 'the world's biggest Christmas cracker'. Measuring about ten feet in length it was brought on to the platform for the traditional presentations of bouquets to be made to missionaries attending the festival. When it was 'pulled' by two Herculean choir members it parted to reveal the bouquets stored inside.

* * *

So Edwin Shepherd entered on the last year of his life. It started quietly, but built up to the sort of climax which made many people think it almost had to be his last year – anything beyond it would have seemed tame by comparison. To begin with there were three more recording sessions at the CTS Studios in March for *The Church's One Foundation*, new arrangements of well-known hymns, the first record made by the choir specifically for the American market. This was the idea of Jesse Peterson of Lillenas, the American music publishers and record producers, who came over to superintend the recording. Three recording sessions were needed to complete the master tape together with several hours of practising the special harmonies and at the end of the three days Jesse Peterson put on record his appreciation of the choir's efforts. 'I have done this with I don't know how many choirs,' he said, 'I would hate to even count them, but I have never come into a choir so well prepared as you were. We don't have the kind of choir that you are in the States. I'm not sure why – maybe we don't have an Edwin Shepherd. I believe England is going to see a tremendous return to music at the local church level and I feel the London Emmanuel Choir will be the real key that unlocks this door.'

A few days after Jesse Peterson returned to the States the choir received its first invitation from the BBC since the early days of its inception to provide a *Sunday Half-Hour* programme on July 19th. The recording took place on Wednesday May 20th at Maida Vale No. 1 Studio. Ronald Allison, the BBC's Court Correspondent and a member of Duke Street Baptist Church, Richmond, provided the linking comments, though these were inserted subsequent to the original recording. The programme's producer, the Rev. W. D. Kennedy Bell was no stranger to choral singing for he had his own choral group, the St. Martin's Singers. Immediately after the broadcast in July a flood of letters descended upon 34 Buckles Way from all parts of the country – and one postcard even from South Africa – from people saying how much they had enjoyed the choir's singing.

Within a week of the BBC recording some 85 members of the choir were on their way to Guernsey for the choir holiday. On the first Sunday Edwin was interviewed by a local journalist, Sam Clap, during the evening service at the Forest Methodist Church and testified to the relevance of his Christian faith in the modern world. On the Wednesday morning they travelled by hydrofoil to the neighbouring island of Jersey and after a drive round the island gave an evening concert at Wesley Grove Methodist Church. After being accommodated overnight in local homes they returned to Guernsey the following day by mail steamer where they sang each night of the week except Wednesday at St. James-the-Less Church. When the time came to leave the island, those who were flying back to the mainland went to the quayside to say farewell to those who were returning by ship. Edwin and Muriel Shepherd were on the quay and as the boat started to pull away from the jetty the whole choir started singing, the music bridging the widening gulf between them as the ship sailed out of the harbour.

Hardly had they returned from Guernsey before Edwin and Muriel were making plans for the 1971 holiday. It was to be a return visit to Llandudno where the choir had previously been in 1954, and they set off for Wales in June to make the necessary arrangements. Their arrival was very different from Edwin's first visit 16 years before. In place of the hurried dash from London by train they were able to take their time visiting friends in various parts of the area by car before arriving in Llandudno from Swansea.

Their first objective was to find bed and breakfast accommodation for themselves for the night. They tried one or two places, and though there was nothing wrong with them and space was available they decided for some reason to look further afield. After trying four establishments they lighted upon a house which was no more distinguished than the rest but which Muriel somehow felt was right.

When they had settled in they enquired of the lady in charge where the Baptist minister lived as this had been their contact last time.

'There isn't a Baptist Church now,' she said. Just then her daughter came in and she turned to her for confirmation, 'There's no Baptist Church now is there? These people are from Banstead and they want to bring a choir down here to sing next year.'

At the mention of a choir the daughter looked at the visitors with renewed interest. 'I'm in touch with a choir from Banstead,' she said, 'the London Emmanuel Choir.'

And with that she rushed upstairs and brought down from her room a Bible. Opening it she withdrew from the fly leaf a little square photograph of Edwin from the choir programme of 1954, which she had cut out and kept as a reminder of the blessing she had received.

Feeling that God had indeed led them to this place they started discussing the person whom it would be best to contact in connection with the choir's visit. The mother was a Welsh Presbyterian and the daughter went to the English Presbyterian Church.

'You ought to go and see our minister,' she said. 'I'm sure he would be able to arrange something.'

Following her directions the Shepherds set off to find the English Presbyterian minister. When they came to what appeared to be the manse they stopped. On the opposite side of the road two men were moving some soil in a garden. One of them came over to see what they wanted.

'We came to see the minister,' they said.

'I'm the minister,' he replied, and then looking at them more closely he paused for a moment as though searching his memory. 'Shepherd,' he said at last, 'Mr. and Mrs. Shepherd isn't it?' Apparently he had been at the Filey Christian Holiday Crusade one year when they were singing and Dr. Sangster had been one of the speakers. They were even more certain of God's guidance when they realised how they had been led to this man, who was only too pleased to offer them the use of his church for the visit the following year.

The next task was to find a hotel big enough to accommodate them and available for the dates they had in mind. They went to the town hall to see the publicity manager and he supplied them with a list of all the biggest hotels in Llandudno.They set off the following day to visit them but each one drew a blank. Most of the hotels had regular bookings from year to year and thus had insufficient spare accommodation to take the choir for the period they wanted. When they had tried the four biggest hotels without success, Muriel turned to Edwin in despair.

'Surely God hasn't opened all these doors for us just to close the final one like this?' she said.

'There's one more hotel we can try,' said Edwin, 'The Seaforth Hotel where we were last time.' They had not tried it earlier because they had thought it would be too small, but when they got there they found the proprietor had taken over the hotel next door and therefore had accommodation to spare. The week before the choir dates was booked and so was the week after but the period the Shepherds wanted was free. So they felt that in a wonderful way God had prepared all the arrangements for the holiday in advance.

All this time plans were proceeding apace for the Fourth Festival of Evangelical Choirs to be held in the autumn. Once again Edwin and Muriel made it their business to acquaint themselves with the choirs taking part, and to go through the music chosen for the festival with them. Looking back Muriel recalls that this was the first time she really enjoyed dashing round the country accompanying the practices. Always a self-effacing person she never looked forward to being prominent among people she didn't know, but somehow the 1970 practices were different.

The festival had orginally been arranged for September 26th that year, but it transpired that this date clashed with two others of considerable importance: the centenary celebrations of the well-known Baptist Church at Duke Street, Richmond, and a proposed series of evangelistic meetings in the Central Hall led by the late Tom Rees under the theme 'Time for Truth'. In the event the latter meetings were never held because of Tom Rees' death earlier in the year, but by that time the date of the Albert Hall Festival had been changed to October 3rd. Was it just a coincidence that this new date was 50 years virtually to the day from that on which Edwin was converted at the Albert Hall under the ministry of the Wood brothers? Coincidence or not it was a very moving moment in the service when he pointed dramatically to the seat where he had been sitting when he gave his heart to Jesus Christ 50 years before.

At one stage the programme appeared to be running a little early so Edwin sprang one of his not infrequent surprises. 'One person in this hall is going to tremble with fear when he hears what the next item is going to be,' he told the audience. 'He has no idea that it is going to happen but I think you will enjoy it nevertheless.' He then turned round and asked Paul Powell, the choir's regular organist who was officiating at the console of the giant Albert Hall organ, to play an organ solo. Paul Powell does not have the letters ARCO after his name for nothing and he took up the challenge in no uncertain terms, treating the delighted audience to a scintillating medley of well-known choruses.

But Edwin was not satisfied. 'Could you manage Widor's Toccata for us, brother?' he called up to the organist. It so happened he had the music with him (after all you could never tell with Edwin) and using the full capacity of the great organ performed the familiar toccata with studied brilliance, finishing in a frenzy of sound, matched only by the thunderous applause which followed.

What the audience did not know was that Edwin's request was the final instalment of an exchange between them that had started at the afternoon rehearsal. Several times during the practice period, Edwin Shepherd had to administer a rebuke to Paul Powell for drowning the choir. When he repeated his request to restrain himself for the fifth time the huge choir collapsed with laughter. It is doubtful if either of them had the last word on that occasion.

One other incident sticks out in Muriel's mind about the festival. Edwin presented her with a bouquet of flowers from himself. It was the first time he had done such a thing at any choir function, and he added a few words of public appreciation for the tremendous help and inspiration she had been to him both at the Albert Hall festivals and throughout the Emmanuel Choir's history.

Almost immediately came another high-spot for the choir and its leader, the 25th anniversary dinner of the choir's foundation at the Criterion restaurant. It was a splendid occasion, with many former choir members reunited with their erstwhile colleagues, and numerous old friends of the choir there to lend their support and offer their congratulations. After all the guests had dined to their satisfaction and the greetings had been read out from those who were not present, Edwin Shepherd rose to speak of the 25 years upon which they were looking back.

'On September 15th, 1945, a historic day dawned,' he said, 'for on that day the choir sang for the first time. I can still recall the thrill of conducting 200 voices for the first time and becoming conscious of the dynamic power they projected into the service. To the glory of God I recall that this same power has been evident for 25 years, culminating in that great service in the Royal Albert Hall last Saturday evening of which one person has just written to us saying, "This letter is to say how grateful we are to God and to the choir for the wonderful evening at the Royal Albert Hall. We were both deeply moved by the evening. The singers themselves were an inspiration, but above all we were very conscious of the presence of Him of whom they sang, so much so that at times we seemed to lose sight of the singers and were conscious, in a way that is hard to put into words, of the deep response in our hearts to the love of Christ and the salvation he came to bring."

'Those are precious words' he continued, 'because they embrace the purpose of what was at the heart of the festival on Saturday. I think we do well on this wonderful evening to record the blessing we have experienced in so many ways throughout our ministry. Despite the many different personalities we are all conscious of a tremendous sense of fellowship in all our activities. This is so strong that many who have left us still feel they belong and support our work in loving prayer.

'Then I have to record the purpose that animates us. It is very true to say that we are people whose hearts are set to serve the Lord. We are prepared to sacrifice time, pleasure and money to carry the Gospel message far and wide. Furthermore it should be recorded that in all the shifting sands of modern theology our faith is firmly based on the Word of God, and it is this unity of faith and purpose which makes such an impact on our audiences every time we sing. It has often been said it is easy to speak after the choir has been singing.

'We look back with deeply grateful hearts on 25 years of wonderful blessing. We are very much a community in which the members pull together in giving willing help whenever needed. There are now only six of our original members still in the choir. There has been a marvellous succession of dedicated singers who have maintained the ministry and handed on the message. We humbly acknowledge the goodness of God and His grace which has brought us to this day.'

Edwin and Muriel Shepherd presented to each choir member a colour photograph of the choir, taken originally for use on the sleeve of their American record, 'The Church's One Foundation', together with a picture of themselves. ('Quite extraordinary' says Muriel in retrospect. 'I couldn't understand at the time why Edwin wanted to give them a photo of us. It was so unlike him to do a thing like that.') Bouquets were presented, scores of commemorative photos were taken, other presentations were made and to crown it all Muriel announced that on the strength of the response to their previous broadcast the BBC had asked the choir to provide another *Sunday Half-Hour* programme, this time at one of the peak listening periods of the year, the Sunday after Christmas. Little did the choir realise at the time the circumstances under which that broadcast would be made.

Towards the end of the evening there occurred a little incident which in retrospect takes on a deeper meaning. Lindsay Glegg conducted the epilogue and in the course of some remarks concerning the blessing that had attended the 25 years' ministry of the choir he jocularly remarked that he was sure he would precede Edwin to Glory. Amid the ensuing laughter Edwin said quietly, 'I'm not so sure about that.'

When they got home that night and were able to relax for the first time for several weeks Edwin looked at his wife, 'Well, my dear,' he said, 'It's complete.'

But of course it wasn't. Already plans for the Carol Festival were well under way. The guest artiste was to be Betty Lou Mills, a Gospel singer who had taken on a new lease of life musically a few years previously when she started singing her own contemporary beat and folk Gospel songs. Edwin was keen to update the style of music at the festivals, but was anxious to do it by evolution, not revolution. He knew that Betty Lou Mills was one of the few people whose contemporary style would be acceptable to the broad mass of his audiences whose musical tastes were decidedly conservative. As it turned out she was not only a tremendous success musically, but a great comfort to Muriel Shepherd in the distressing events of the Carol Festival.

He also planned to introduce a group of young people who belonged to the Evangelical Church of the Deaf, who were to express the words of two pieces in sign language while the choir sang. He was most enthusiastic about this, having been thrilled and deeply moved by a visit he paid to the group earlier in the year at the invitation of their leader Albert Barritt. Edwin did not live to see them perform at the festival but they came to one of the choir rehearsals at the Bridewell Hall a few weeks before the festival to practice their part with the choir. At the end of the evening he spoke to them through their interpreter, telling them tenderly how they would in effect be evangelising with the choir. It was a most moving experience for those present.

A long-playing record was being produced of the Albert Hall festival and at the beginning of November Edwin was asked to go along to the Granada studios in Kennington while they were editing the four-track master tape to produce the two-track stereo recording required. It so happened that the tonal balance of the opening verses of the first hymn was not quite what it should have been, and as Edwin was there the recording manager asked him to record an introduction to the festival which they subsequently superimposed over the first hymn, little realising that within a few days of the record being released his voice would be heard no more.

At the end of the month he paid his last visit to the Royal Albert Hall, to conduct an augmented Emmanuel Choir leading the singing of the Battle Hymn of the Republic at the 'Freedom and Faith' rally to commemorate the 350th anniversary of the sailing of the Pilgrim Fathers to America. Billy Graham was the speaker and the programme was full of rich pageantry.

He was also making plans for the Spring Festival of 1971 by this time, plans that would, he hoped, take the development of the choir one stage further than it had so far reached. He had been introduced to the work of an American composer, Susan Jaeger and an arranger, Don Blackley, who had produced a series of choir pieces under the general title 'Folk with Feeling', introducing a rhythmic beat and percussion accompaniment which gave the music a contemporary twist without diminishing the significance of the words. This seemed to him to be the right sort of step forward for the choir.

He was as aware as anyone of changing musical tastes and particularly of the need to provide music which would both enthuse the younger people in the choir and also appeal to younger members of the audience without upsetting unnecessarily the older supporters of the choir.

For the same reasons he had always been keen to start a guitar group in the choir. As long ago as 1961, a group of twelve girls were asked to get together and form a group, but for one reason and another they never managed to get very far and the idea died a natural death. As time went on various individuals in the choir took up the guitar and some of them sang solo items at choir performances accompanying themselves on the guitar, but Edwin was still keen to get a group going, so he approached Susan Allum, one of the guitar players, and asked her if she would lead such a group. She agreed, and the necessary number of guitarists were forthcoming from the choir.

Towards the middle of November the group met for its first practice, which went very well. Susan phoned Edwin Shepherd the next day and said, 'Believe it or not we seem to be able to play.'

'Good,' he replied. 'When can I come over and hear you?'

'Well, I know you're terribly busy,' she said, 'with the festival in three weeks time, how about leaving it until after Christmas? We'll have another couple of practices and then sometime in January . . .'

'No, I want to hear you now,' he interrupted.

'Our next practice is in a fortnight's time,' said Susan.

'I'll be there,' he said, and he was. It was exactly a week before he collapsed on the platform at the Central Hall. He was overjoyed at what he heard. This had always been one of his ambitions within the choir, and when he got home that night he was, Muriel recalls, 'walking on air'. They gave their first performance at the Spring Festival of 1971 so he never heard them perform publicly but it was just one more of those little incidents which came to have greater significance after he died, that at his own insistence and in the face of considerable reluctance on the part of those involved he was able to satisfy himself that the group had established itself before he passed on.

On the Monday before the Carol Festival Father Christmas, alias John Cook, came to see him to collect his accordion which had been repaired and to discuss final arrangements for Wednesday's performance. He was to pull the Christmas sleigh on to the platform with the young daughter of two of the choir members on it dressed as a fairy. He would introduce her to the audience, chat for a minute or two and then get her to reveal the missionary bouquets on the sleigh. It was all settled, and as John said goodbye to Edwin at the door he said, 'Not to worry if it doesn't go quite right on Wednesday. We'll treat that as a rehearsal and make it right for Thursday.'

'No, let's make the last one perfect,' said Edwin.

Was it a slip of the tongue, or did he have some strange premonition that within 48 hours he would be called home, as Muriel put it in a subsequent letter 'straight from conducting the London Emmanuel Choir to conducting a heavenly choir'? No one will ever know this side of eternity but one thing is certain he died as he would have wanted to die, in harness, and among those he knew and loved so well.

Chapter 8

THE MAN AND HIS MUSIC

A character assessment of Edwin Shepherd must begin with all the superlatives, for he earned them. He was, first and foremost, a man of God. He had a very deep personal relationship with his Maker which was the most important thing in his life. He loved the Bible, knew its message, thrilled to its promises and accepted its challenges. He was a man of prayer, not only in public, but more importantly in private. No major decision was ever taken until it had been saturated in prayer, and no task once started was out of his prayers until it was successfully completed. The contrast between the formal, aloof atmosphere of the established church when he was a choirboy, and the exuberant, uninhibited spirit he met among his early Pentecostal friends produced in him not only just the right balance between the two extremes, but also made him tolerant of any and every manifestation of true Christian faith no matter the externals of denomination or churchmanship.

He was an evangelist in the fullest sense of that much misused word. He had a real longing to introduce men and women to his own Saviour and Lord, but was never one to force his beliefs on others. Those who worked for him for 42 years in the bank did not avoid being alone with him for fear that he would harangue them about their sin. His was the positive approach—showing forth in his everyday relationships the love of Christ which he had experienced in his own life.

He was a hard worker—indeed he seems to have been one of those people who work harder the longer they live. Any man who can hold down a responsible job while at the same time exercising pastoral responsibility for a local church, as Edwin did from 1937–45, must by any yardstick be a hard worker. Edwin lived 20 miles away from the church for which he was responsible, thus multiplying his workload well beyond the average man's capacity. But it was good training for his later dual role of bank official and part-time choir conductor—and his even more strenuous task of full-time conductor on his retirement.

He had a great sense of humour. Visualise Edwin Shepherd and you see him smiling. Listen to him and you hear him laughing. It was an infectious laugh, utterly necessary in dealing with the varied temperaments and personalities which made up his choir. And it was spontaneous, bursting out in unexpected places. He was not the sort of man who switched off his smile in private. The whole of his life was permeated by a sense of fun, an awareness of the ridiculous in any situation and a desire to share his enjoyment with others.

He was a born leader. No one could have held the choir together for 25 years unless they had the instinct for leadership. It is true that his powers of leadership were more evident in his choir work than at the bank, but he never made any secret of the fact that he wanted no advancement in the bank which would curtail the amount of time outside office hours he could spend in other service for God. He himself described his leadership of the choir as that of a 'benevolent dictator'—which after all is the most effective form of government. It is difficult to imagine a choir being conducted by a committee, and obviously he had to make the decisions so far as the conducting was concerned and they had to be obeyed. But as the ministry and effectiveness of the choir has grown and the organisation become more complex there have been those who have felt that on matters of concern to the choir there should be more consultation with members. But his view was that he had been called to lead the choir and choir members had been called to follow and he was genuinely disturbed when his attitude was not understood or accepted.

He was a humble, self-effacing man. This was the quality which balanced his leadership. There was, it is true, something of the showman about him, but that was because he liked a spectacle. It was never centred around him personally, though naturally as the choir's leader he inevitably enjoyed much of the limelight. He sincerely sought in all he did to divert attention from himself to his Lord. Sometimes at choir practices he would thank the choir for 'putting up with' him and suffering his 'human frailty'; he was very conscious of his weaknesses.

He was a perfectionist. Everything had to be just right, so far as he was concerned, whether it was the straight edge of the garden lawn or the orderly precision of the choir's entry. (In this latter connection one wonders how many members of the audience, when they see the choir file on to the platform as though they have been practising all afternoon, realise, that, other than at the Central Hall festivals, ten minutes earlier they will have had no idea in what order they are to enter? Such is the disciplined professionalism of the choir that it takes no more than a few minutes to sort them out and allocate positions.) Edwin's quest for perfection did not make it easy for those nearest him, for a perfectionist is intolerant of anything which falls below that standard. This was a good thing in that it kept his sights high and never allowed him to rest on his laurels—two weeks before his death when he and Muriel were listening with a friend to the final edited tape of the fourth Albert Hall festival, his reaction was 'It has got to go on improving'; but it tended to make him very wary of delegating responsibility to others, thus increasing the burden of his own responsibilities.

He had time for people. He was never too busy to see a member of the choir if they had a problem they wanted to discuss with him. Not only choir members; on one occasion when he returned from an engagement thoroughly worn out he had a call from a neighbour living a few doors down the road whose little daughter was seriously ill. Without waiting for refreshment, or to have a rest, he went straight to his neighbour's home and there prayed with the family. Many choir members tell of numerous times when he took them to one side and listened to their anxieties and concerns, or when he showed in other ways the value and worth he placed upon each individual member of the choir.

He was a good husband. For nearly 37 years he and Muriel were a mutual strength and comfort to each other, but he always made it plain that his highest loyalty was to his Lord. When they were married he said to her, 'We'll always put the Lord first and His service,' and Muriel confirms that this was always so. 'He never allowed anything to stand in the way of service to the Lord. If there was a family celebration or some outing planned and then a call came to serve the Lord everything else had to be put aside.' But such an attitude in no way diminished his love and concern for Muriel. 'If I had any problem concerning the Word of God I asked him and he would explain it to me. If I had a burden he would always pray with me. If I was ill he would always lay his hands on me and pray for me. I have never known him turn aside from his Christian experience. Not only to me but to all my family he has been a great blessing.'

Naturally, as each was possessed of a strong character there were occasional disagreements (and they used to rib each other unmercifully at choir rehearsals on occasions) but on major matters they were invariably as one. Certainly their relationship needed to be a strong and stable one to withstand the pressures under which Edwin worked. They had no children of their own—and yet in a very real sense the choir members were their family, all 150 of them and more, and they had the same concern for them that they would have for their own flesh and blood, visiting them when they were ill, attending weddings, celebrating birthdays and caring about the trivia of family relationships—and as for the choir's weekend visits to the provinces they were more like a family outing to the coast.

Last, but hardly least, he was of course a musician. His early choral training, together with his natural musical ability enabled him to develop a fine solo voice, but music was always for him a vehicle of praise and testimony, and it is this concept which underlay all his subsequent achievements. Music was of no value in his view unless it was fulfilling a purpose and he always urged the choir never to let the words become subservient to the music. In the precise sense it cannot be said of him that he was a great musician—Muriel Shepherd has better qualifications in the technical field—but if greatness in a musician lies in interpreting the music to his audience and helping to achieve its purpose, then Edwin was the greatest.

Only those who have sung under his conducting can adequately describe why he was able to elicit such a response from them. Even then no form of words will really suffice. He seemed to *live* the piece of music, and the hours of practice and rehearsal gave the choir one voice—his voice—which he controlled not by operating a sort of corporate larynx but by facial expressions, gestures of the hands, his posture and movements.

But these in themselves would not have been enough. The choir responded to him because they loved him, because they knew at first hand his radiant Christian personality, his humility, his zest and energy, his constant demand for perfection, his sense of fun—they loved him because he loved his Lord, and the love shone transparently through everything they sang.

In this context a discussion of his style of music is irrelevant. Obviously no useful purpose is served by limiting a choir's repertoire to music which is hackneyed and out of date, nor by following regardless the popular trend of the day. Any choirmaster must be the judge of exactly where within the wide spectrum of music his contribution lies. What Edwin Shepherd had—and what many other conductors would give their right arm for—was the power to project his own personality, greatly magnified through the choir, to his audience. And because his personality was totally dedicated to the God he worshipped the choir in a very real sense had 'God with them' when they sang. His last word to them would surely have been 'Sing Emmanuel'.

POSTSCRIPT

The London Emmanuel Choir is alive and well and living in South East England. The loss of their founder and conductor has brought no curtailment of their activities nor diminution in their popularity. The choir is in fact functioning under Muriel Shepherd very much as it would have done under Edwin had he been alive, continuing the cautious move towards more contemporary styles of music without abandoning its more traditional repertoire.

Attendances at the 1971 Spring Festival fully justified the trustees' decision not to curtail the three performances, as some had recommended. (Nearly £3,000 was raised through offerings at the festival, the memorial service and a subsequent rally towards the cost of a specially constructed boat, called the m.v. Emmanuel as a tribute to Edwin, for the Far East Broadcasting Association's Christian radio station in the Seychelles. The choir has supported the association financially since the work of Donal and Mabel Glegg, with the Africa Missionary Fellowship in Rhodesia, who had received as much as £1,000 a year through the choir's support since 1955, came to an end a few years ago.)

It seems that the choir and its new leader have taken the traumatic events of Christmas 1970 more or less in their stride, and many will feel that the manner and timing of Edwin's death had something to do with this, together with the volume of prayer which arose from believing Christian people during those weeks. It was one more indication, if such were needed, of the guidance and blessing of God which the choir has experienced throughout its life so far, and which it will assuredly continue to enjoy in the future.

APPENDIX

RECORDS OF THE LONDON EMMANUEL CHOIR

Singles (78 r.p.m.)	**Released**
Jesu, lover of my soul; When I survey the wondrous cross. (E)	*1950*
There is a green hill; There is a fountain filled with blood. (E)	*1950*
Rock of ages; How sweet the name of Jesus sounds. (E)	*1950*
Burdens are lifted at Calvary; Ivory palaces. (P)	*1955*
The Lord's my shepherd, He lives. (P)	*1955*
Go down Moses; Don't stop praying; On my journey home; Do you love my Lord? (P)	*1955*
How sweet the name of Jesus sounds; Laudamus. (P)	*1957*
O worship the King; Thine be the glory. (P)	*1957*
No room for the baby; The Lord's my shepherd. (E)	*1959*
Lead us Heavenly Father, lead us; O perfect love. (E)	*1959*
At even ere the sun was set; I will sing of my redeemer. (E)	*1960*

Extended play (45 r.p.m.)

How Great Thou Art (R) *1961*

Down from His Glory (P) *1961*
Gospel bells; Down from His glory; The love of God; At even ere the sun was set.

Christmas Carols (P) *1961*
Christians awake; See, amid the winter's snow; Good Christian men rejoice; It came upon a midnight clear.

Heaven Came Down (P) *1965*
Heaven came down; Since I have been redeemed; Sound the battle cry; Mine eyes have seen the glory.

Above All Else (P) *1967*
O Church of God; Above all else; This is my Father's world; Jesus, Thy blood and righteousness.

Long play ($33\frac{1}{3}$ r.p.m.)

London Emmanuel Choir (P: reissued as *Festival Songs*) *1958*
I love Him; The unveiled Christ; We shall rise; All in the April evening; Down in the valley; No one understands like Jesus; Somebody's knocking at my door; Take my life.

Christmas Joy (P: reissued twice: QLP4) *1960*
Christians awake; See, amid the winter's snow; The first nowell; It came upon the midnight clear; While shepherds watched their flocks; Joy to the world; Good Christian men, rejoice; Once in royal David's city; Hark! the Herald angels sing; Who is He in yonder stall?

Came Carolling (S: reissued: SHLP1204) *1962*
Hark, the herald angels sing; Christmas morn is dawning; No room in the inn; An angel brought it down; Little King Jesus; He is born; O Holy night; O come all ye faithful; All hail Emmanuel; Masters in this hall; Away in the manger; Once in royal David's city; Ding dong merrily on high; While shepherds watched their flocks; The first nowell; There's a song in the air; Worthy is the Lamb.

Festival Favourites (H) *1963*
Come Thou almighty King; Boundless salvation; Yes He can; When I survey the wondrous cross; O for a closer walk with God; Yes He did; Go down Moses; O Light of Life; Near the cross.

Ring the Bells (H) *1964*
Ring the bells; When the Lord of Love was born; Look away to Bethlehem; It was a night of wonder; No room; So long ago; Gloria in excelsis deo; Rocking; Long ago; Jesus, Jesus, rest for your head; Rise up shepherd and foller; In a cave.

Praise and Rejoice (P: reissued as KLP 26) *1965*
Canticle of praise; The Beatitudes; Jesu, priceless treasure; Love found a way; How can you reject Him?; Lord, I want a diadem; O for a thousand tongues; How sweet the name of Jesus sounds; Peace; The ninety and nine; Only one life; Jesus lives!

Give God the Glory (P) *1966*
Praise the God of Abraham; All in an April evening; Rise, shine; I waited for the Lord; Saviour, Thy children keep; I believe in miracles; The morning trumpet; The unveiled Christ; The Lord's my shepherd; Amen; Jesus is coming again; Let us break bread together; Onward, Christian soldiers.

Carolling, Carolling (P) *1966*
Sing we of the Saviour; In the bleak mid-winter; Hush-a-bye Bethlehem babe; Carol of the bells; The little road to Bethlehem; Christ born to be Saviour; Yule fantasy; Carolling, carolling; I wonder as I wander; The ballad of Bethlehem; Go tell it on the mountain; The love that heaven sent down; At the first coming of the Lord; O holy night.

Whispering Hope, with Westminster Sinfonia Orchestra (P: JLP 147) *1968*
Never fades the name of Jesus; Can there be one; O Saviour mine; Whispering hope; Lord Jesus, think on me; It is well with my soul; Far out on the desolate billow; One day I walked along a country road; The Lord's my shepherd; Jesu, joy of man's desiring; How great Thou art.

Born a King (P: JLP 157) *1968*
Christmas cantata composed by John W. Peterson, with soloists.

Let the Whole World Know, with Westminster Sinfonia Orchestra (P: JLPS 162) *1969*
Let the whole world know; There is more to life; He's everything to me; Listen to the lambs; Go tell it on the mountain; God's choir; Jesus was praying for me; Soon ah will be done; Sooner or later; Ye shall be witnesses.

Heaven Came Down (P: reissue of tracks from earlier EPs: QLP 9) *1970*
Heaven came down; This is my Father's world; Hark! my soul*; Look and live†; At even ere the sun was set; Sound the battle cry; Jesus, Thy blood and righteousness; Great is my joy*; Noah†; Down from His glory. (*Solo: Marion Redwood; †male voice quintet.)

The Church's One Foundation (P: JLPS 170) *1971*
Let all the people praise Thee; O worship the King; Arise, my soul, arise; Be still, my soul; Begin, my tongue, some heavenly theme; The Church's one foundation; Come, Thou long-expected Jesus; Open my eyes, that I may see; They that wait upon the Lord; Do you know the love of Jesus?; God is in every tomorrow; Crown Him with many crowns.

Emmanuel, live recording of 1970 Carol Festival (P: JLPS 171) *1971*
Everywhere Christmas tonight; Bell carol; The song of the shepherds; Emmanuel – God with us; It came upon a midnight clear; O come, O come Emmanuel; Christmas song; Tiny little baby boy; The minor carol; Christmas prayer; Hallelujah! Hallelujah!; How great Thou art; plus "Carols by Candelight" and congregational carols.

ASSOCIATED RECORDS

LONDON EMMANUEL CHOIR MALE VOICE QUINTET

Extended play

Jubilee! (P) 1965
My God is real; The happy jubilee; I want my life to tell for Jesus; I'm a-trampin'.

Look and Live! (P) *1966*
Look and live!; Jesus, the very thought of Thee; Roll, billows, roll; Noah, Amen.

MARION REDWOOD

Extended play

Hark! My Soul (P) *1965*
Somebody sang a wonderful song; Hark! my soul, it is the Lord; Keep a song ringing in your heart; God cannot lie; Great is my joy.

Long play

Wonderful Story, with London Emmanuel Choir and Westminster Sinfonia Strings (P: JLPS 165) *1969*

The big story; I'll tell the world; When God speaks; Holy Lord of Hosts; Wonderful story; Beside still waters; The great I am; The everlasting arms; Fierce raged the tempest; He whispered 'Peace be still'; Jesus Saviour, pilot me; I'll go with God; How wonderful art Thou.

ROYAL ALBERT HALL CHOIR FESTIVALS

Long play

Second Festival of Evangelical Mixed Voice Choirs (T) *1964*

Volume 1. Guide us O Thou Great Jehovah; Heaven came down; A flag to follow; Close to Thee; Christ is all; And the Glory of the Lord; Hail Thou once despised Jesus; Since my Saviour found me; Fairest Lord Jesus; He the pearly gates will open; Jesu, lover of my soul.

Volume 2. Sound the battle cry; Bring in the sheaves; O, the love that wilt not let me go; O, Light of Life; The day of God is breaking; God Himself is with us; O Lord I'm coming home; plus address by Lindsay Glegg.

Third Festival of Evangelical Choirs (P: JLP 153) *1968*

Praise ye the Lord of Hosts; It is well with my soul; O how I love Jesus; Hiding in the shadow of the rock; Jesus, name I love; Lift up your hearts; All creatures of our God and King; My heart's prayer; His own; When Jesus whispers 'Peace'; Let Thy mantle fall; plus congregational singing, male quintet and soloists.

Fourth Festival of Evangelical Choirs (P: JLPS 169) *1970*

All glory to Jesus; He's everything to me; Substitution; It was early in the morning; The love of God; Far beyond all human comprehension; A name I highly treasure; We're marching to Zion; Let the whole world know; Contentment in His Love; Over the sunset mountains; None other Lamb, Come, Thou fount of ev'ry blessing; Deep down in my heart; Behold He cometh; plus congregational singing and introduction by Edwin Shepherd.

Notes:

The record publishers are indicated thus:
E – Evangelical Recordings;
P – Pilgrim Recordings;
R – Redemption Records;
H – Herald Recordings;
S – Sharon Recordings;
T – Teldisc.
Most of the records published before 1966 are discontinued; only those records carrying a reference number in the list above were still available at the time of publication of this book.